DORLING KINDERSLEY ⬚ EYEWITNESS BOOKS

DINOSAUR

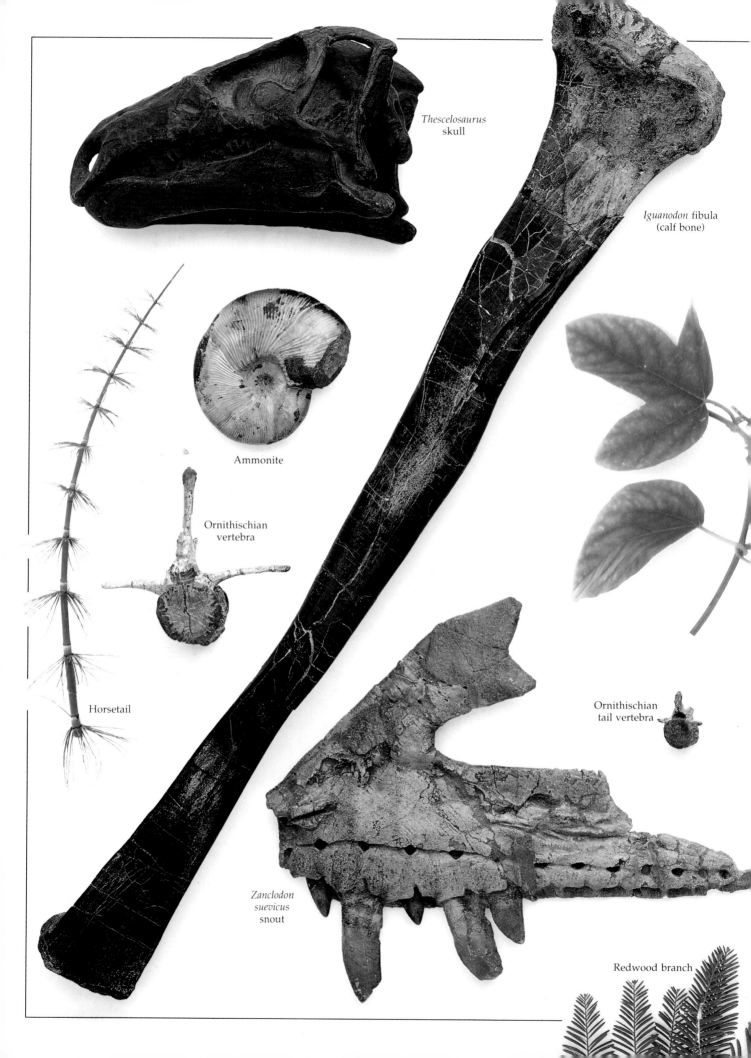

Thescelosaurus skull

Iguanodon fibula (calf bone)

Ammonite

Ornithischian vertebra

Horsetail

Ornithischian tail vertebra

Zanclodon suevicus snout

Redwood branch

Chirostenotes
claw

Stegosaur
tooth

Dogwood
leaves

DK EYEWITNESS BOOKS

DINOSAUR

Written by
DAVID NORMAN, Ph.D.,
AND
ANGELA MILNER, Ph.D.

Passionflower
leaves

Gizzard
stones

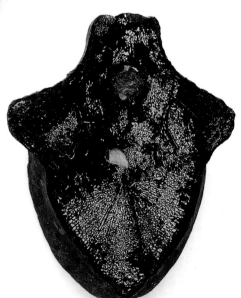

Cross section of
Iguanodon tail vertebra

Albertosaurus
claw

Hadrosaur teeth

Megalosaurus
tooth

DK

Dorling Kindersley

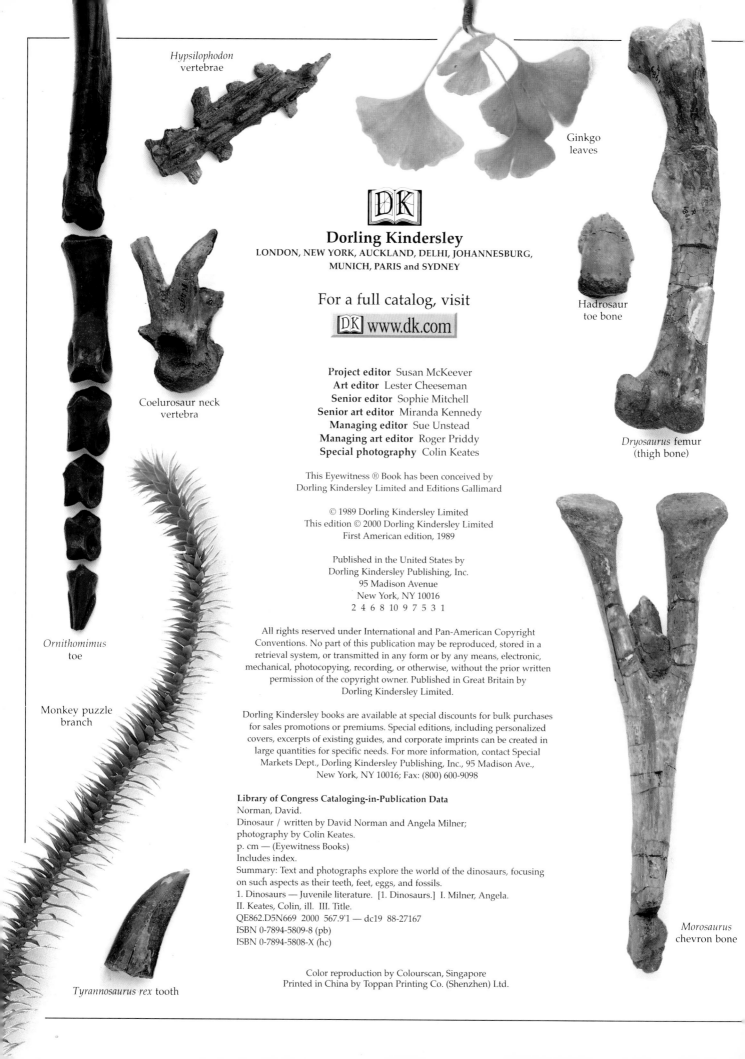

Hypsilophodon
vertebrae

Ginkgo
leaves

Coelurosaur neck
vertebra

Hadrosaur
toe bone

DK

Dorling Kindersley
LONDON, NEW YORK, AUCKLAND, DELHI, JOHANNESBURG,
MUNICH, PARIS and SYDNEY

For a full catalog, visit
DK www.dk.com

Project editor Susan McKeever
Art editor Lester Cheeseman
Senior editor Sophie Mitchell
Senior art editor Miranda Kennedy
Managing editor Sue Unstead
Managing art editor Roger Priddy
Special photography Colin Keates

This Eyewitness ® Book has been conceived by
Dorling Kindersley Limited and Editions Gallimard

© 1989 Dorling Kindersley Limited
This edition © 2000 Dorling Kindersley Limited
First American edition, 1989

Published in the United States by
Dorling Kindersley Publishing, Inc.
95 Madison Avenue
New York, NY 10016
2 4 6 8 10 9 7 5 3 1

Dorling Kindersley books are available at special discounts for bulk purchases
for sales promotions or premiums. Special editions, including personalized
covers, excerpts of existing guides, and corporate imprints can be created in
large quantities for specific needs. For more information, contact Special
Markets Dept., Dorling Kindersley Publishing, Inc., 95 Madison Ave.,
New York, NY 10016; Fax: (800) 600-9098

Dryosaurus femur
(thigh bone)

Library of Congress Cataloging-in-Publication Data
Norman, David.
Dinosaur / written by David Norman and Angela Milner;
photography by Colin Keates.
p. cm — (Eyewitness Books)
Includes index.
Summary: Text and photographs explore the world of the dinosaurs, focusing
on such aspects as their teeth, feet, eggs, and fossils.
1. Dinosaurs — Juvenile literature. [1. Dinosaurs.] I. Milner, Angela.
II. Keates, Colin, ill. III. Title.
QE862.D5N669 2000 567.9'1 — dc19 88-27167
ISBN 0-7894-5809-8 (pb)
ISBN 0-7894-5808-X (hc)

Ornithomimus
toe

Monkey puzzle
branch

Color reproduction by Colourscan, Singapore
Printed in China by Toppan Printing Co. (Shenzhen) Ltd.

Tyrannosaurus rex tooth

Morosaurus
chevron bone

Contents

Heterodontosaurus skull

What were the dinosaurs?

BACK IN THE MISTS OF TIME, there lived an extraordinary group of animals called dinosaurs. They survived for nearly 150 million years, and then disappeared off the face of the Earth in the most mysterious extinction ever. Many of them were gigantic, and some were no bigger than a chicken. Some were peaceful and ate only plants; others were fierce sharp-toothed flesh eaters. Dinosaurs were reptiles, just like the living iguana lizard on this page. They had scaly skin and laid eggs. But unlike the lizard, which has short, sprawling legs, dinosaurs had long legs tucked under their bodies, which meant that they could move much more efficiently. Many other reptiles shared the dinosaur world, swimming in the sea and flying in the air, but dinosaurs lived only on land. We know about them today because their bones and teeth have been preserved in rock as fossils.

HIPS CAN TELL A STORY
Dinosaurs fall into two main groups, according to the structure of their hipbones. Saurischian, or "lizard-hipped" dinosaurs, had hips in which the two lower bones pointed in opposite directions. Ornithischian, or "bird-hipped" dinosaurs, had the two lower hipbones lying together behind the back leg.

Tyrannosaurus rex (lizard-hipped)

Hipbones separate (saurischian)

Iguanodon (bird-hipped)

Hipbones next to each other (ornithischian)

Iguana lizard

DINOSAURS COULDN'T FLY!
Flying reptiles, like the pterosaurs shown here feeding on a *Triceratops* carcass, shared the dinosaur world, but were not dinosaurs. No dinosaur could fly.

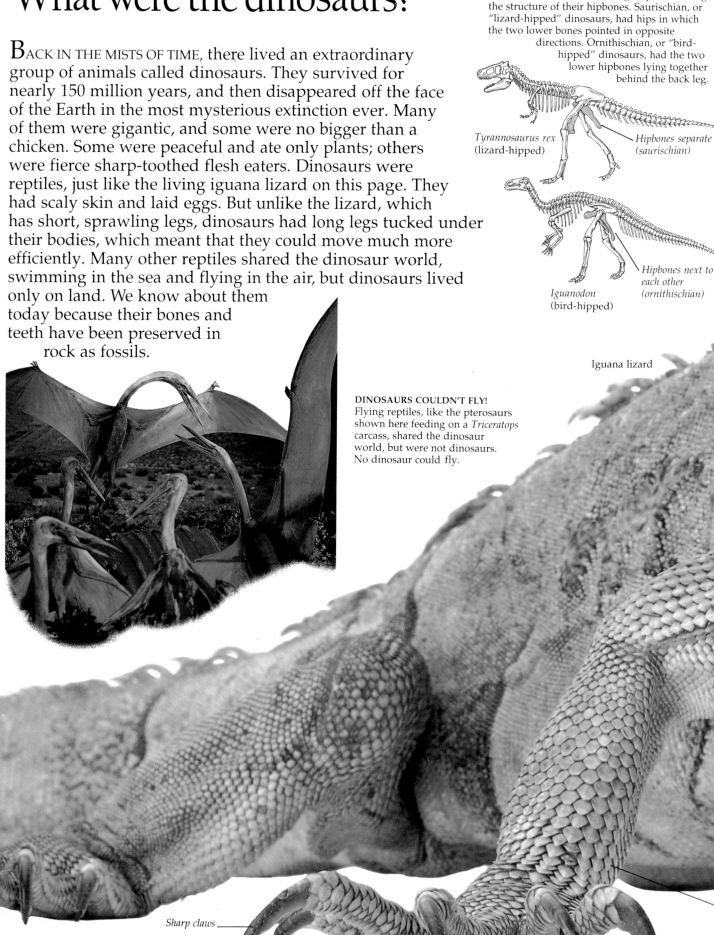

Sharp claws

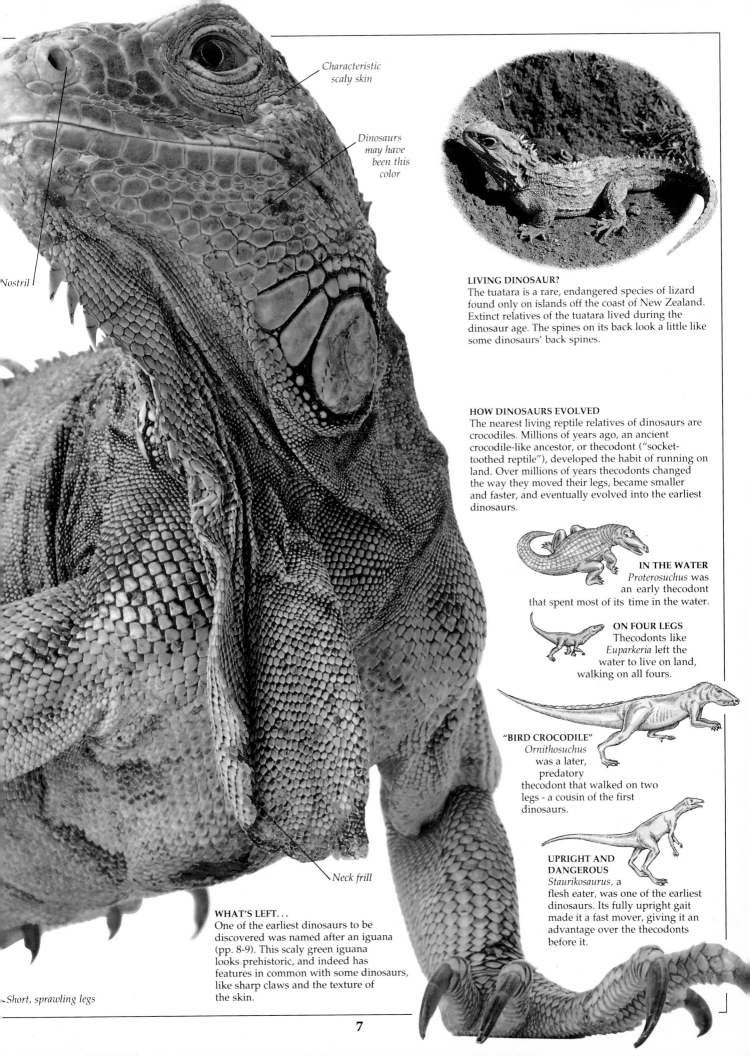

Characteristic scaly skin

Dinosaurs may have been this color

Nostril

LIVING DINOSAUR?
The tuatara is a rare, endangered species of lizard found only on islands off the coast of New Zealand. Extinct relatives of the tuatara lived during the dinosaur age. The spines on its back look a little like some dinosaurs' back spines.

HOW DINOSAURS EVOLVED
The nearest living reptile relatives of dinosaurs are crocodiles. Millions of years ago, an ancient crocodile-like ancestor, or thecodont ("socket-toothed reptile"), developed the habit of running on land. Over millions of years thecodonts changed the way they moved their legs, became smaller and faster, and eventually evolved into the earliest dinosaurs.

IN THE WATER
Proterosuchus was an early thecodont that spent most of its time in the water.

ON FOUR LEGS
Thecodonts like _Euparkeria_ left the water to live on land, walking on all fours.

"BIRD CROCODILE"
Ornithosuchus was a later, predatory thecodont that walked on two legs - a cousin of the first dinosaurs.

UPRIGHT AND DANGEROUS
Staurikosaurus, a flesh eater, was one of the earliest dinosaurs. Its fully upright gait made it a fast mover, giving it an advantage over the thecodonts before it.

Neck frill

WHAT'S LEFT...
One of the earliest dinosaurs to be discovered was named after an iguana (pp. 8-9). This scaly green iguana looks prehistoric, and indeed has features in common with some dinosaurs, like sharp claws and the texture of the skin.

Short, sprawling legs

Early discoveries

Iguanodon tooth from lower jaw

ALTHOUGH DINOSAUR remains have been around for millions of years, people knew nothing about these extraordinary creatures until the last century. One of the first people to discover dinosaur bones was an English doctor named Gideon Mantell, who collected rocks and fossils as a hobby. In 1820 Dr. Mantell, with his wife, Mary Ann, found some large teeth embedded in stone. Mantell had never seen teeth quite like them before. And when he found some bones nearby, he began to do some serious research. After a lot of work, Dr. Mantell concluded that the teeth and bones had belonged to some kind of giant reptile which he named *Iguanodon*, meaning "Iguana tooth" (pp. 6-7). Two other giant reptiles were discovered in England soon afterward, named *Megalosaurus* and *Hylaeosaurus*. But it was not until 1841 that these creatures were given a group name. Sir Richard Owen, a well-known scientist of the time, declared that they should be called "dinosaurs," meaning "terrible lizards." And so began a time of great excitement in the scientific world. The great dinosaur hunt began all over the world.

Worn edge

Tooth from upper jaw

THE FIRST TEETH
Still embedded in the gritty stone in which they were found by the Mantells are the original *Iguanodon* teeth. The top edges of the dinosaur' teeth were worn down by the plants it chewed. (pp. 26-27).

Horn on nose was actually a thumb spike

Long whiplash tail like an iguana lizard

A ROUGH SKETCH
Dr. Mantell had discovered a collection of bones and teeth. But what on earth had the owner of the bones looked like when it was alive? Mantell pictured it as a gigantic lizard, a bit like an iguana. He drew a picture of it perched on a branch, with its thumb spike (of which he had found only one) placed on its nose!

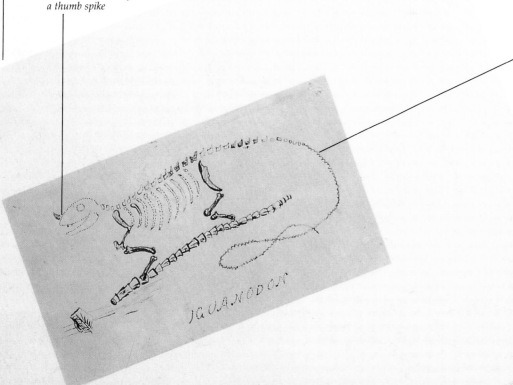

Gideon Mantell's original drawing of *Iguanodon*

8

Part of an *Iguanodon* backbone

Backbones fused together

MYSTERY BONE

MYSTERY BONE
In 1809, long before the word "dinosaur" had been heard of, a man named William Smith found some bones in Sussex, England, including this shinbone. At the time, he did not realize what they were. Only later were they identified as belonging to *Iguanodon*.

THE DISCOVERER
Although he was a medical doctor by profession, Gideon Mantell was an enthusiastic collector of rocks and fossils. As his collection grew, his home began to look like a museum.

MORE BONES
More bones from *Iguanodon* found by Gideon Mantell include this portion of the backbone which fitted between the hips of the animal.

DINNER IN A DINOSAUR
As the interest in dinosaurs grew, a great display of giant models was mounted in the gardens of London's Crystal Palace. Before the *Iguanodon* model was finished, the sculptor held a dinner party for 20 people inside it.

Iguanodon tibia (shinbone)

MONSTERS IN THE PARK
These two concrete models of *Iguanodon* were made by the sculptor Benjamin Waterhouse Hawkins in the last century. Although inaccurate - *Iguanodon* looked nothing like this (p. 39) - they can be seen to this day in the park at the Crystal Palace, London.

Dinosaur landscape

Monkey puzzle:
Araucaria araucana

DINOSAURS LIVED on Earth for nearly 150 million years, and it is not surprising that their world changed substantially during this time. Continents, at first just one great landmass, gradually drifted apart until they resembled the modern arrangement that we are familiar with. This meant that the climate changed as well, and both these factors influenced the types of plants that grew. These changes happened slowly over millions of years and animals adapted accordingly. At the beginning of the dinosaur age, the landscape was covered with low shrubby fern-like plants. Then came a time when huge evergreen forests and groves of cycads flourished. Later on, the first flowering plants added color to the scene. Many plants and flowers that the dinosaurs may have eaten can still be seen growing today.

FIR FEAST
Herbivorous dinosaurs had enough vegetation to satisfy their appetites. Duckbilled dinosaurs, such as *Parasaurolophus*, above, could cope with tough plants because their jaws and teeth were so powerful. Even fir needles posed no problem.

ANCIENT PUZZLE
Living monkey puzzle trees are relatives of ones which grew long before dinosaurs ever walked the Earth.

CYCAD FROND
Cycads were abundant during most of the dinosaur reign, and, though very rare, can still be found today.

A DINOSAUR HOME
This scene shows the type of landscape that would have been familiar to dinosaurs of about 130 million years ago. Horsetails, ferns, and cycads are everywhere.

Conifer:
Pseudotsuga menziesii

Passionflower:
Passiflora sp.

Holly:
Ilex aquifolium

Cycad:
Cycas revoluta

THE FLOWERING
The first flowering plant appeared during the last period of the dinosaurs' reign. Flowering plants can reproduce more quickly than other types, and they rapidly came to dominate plant communities worldwide. Flowers introduced color and variety into the diets of dinosaurs .

A MAGNOLIA
It is surprising to think of dinosaurs eating flowers, but when magnolias appeared about 100 million years ago they were no doubt munched on by many plant-eating dinosaurs.

Ginkgo:
Ginkgo biloba

English Laurel:
Prunus laurocerasus
"Otto Luykeres"

Magnolia:
Magnolia loebneri

FERN FEEDER
Dinosaurs such as *Stegosaurus* fed on low-growing vegetation like ferns (p. 34). Others, such as the long-necked sauropods, tackled the tougher vegetation of the high conifer forests and cycad groves.

Fern:
Marattia werneri

Fern:
Blechnum sp.

Horsetail:
Equisetum giganteum

Dogwood:
Cornus alba

Little and large

A LOT OF PEOPLE think of dinosaurs as being massive creatures, big enough to reach the treetops. But there were also tiny dinosaurs, ones that would not even reach your knee. The biggest creatures ever to walk the Earth were the sauropod group of dinosaurs, which were all plant eaters. *Brachiosaurus* was the biggest sauropod that we know much about. It weïghed about 70 tons, was 70 ft (22 m) long, and stood 39 ft (12 m) high - about as tall as a four-story building or a big oak tree. Bones have recently been found belonging to dinosaurs that may have been even larger than *Brachiosaurus*. They were named *Supersaurus* and *Ultrasaurus* and they may have been a third larger than *Brachiosaurus*!

When alive, *Ultrasaurus* would have weighed as much as 20 large elephants. In contrast with these peaceful giants, the tiny dinosaurs like *Compsognathus* (far right) were mostly agile, crafty meat eaters, some no heavier than a cat.

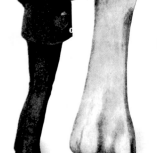

AS TALL AS A HOUSE
This French engraving shows a popular image of dinosaurs as giants: an alarming visitor to a Paris street investigates a balcony on the fifth floor of a tall building.

THE OWNER OF THE BONE
This *Brachiosaurus* is the type of dinosaur that owned the massive leg bone (far right). The huge, pillar-like forelimbs were longer than the hind limbs - probably to help it reach up to the treetops for food.

FANTASTIC FEMUR
The femur (upper leg bone) shown at right belonged to a *Brachiosaurus*. If you stood next to a *Brachiosaurus* leg, you would hardly reach past its knee bone! The gentleman (left) is examining an *Apatosaurus* femur, which measures 6 ft 10 in (2.1 m) long. *Apatosaurus* was another type of sauropod dinosaur.

Part of a large *Brachiosaurus* femur, ending in knee joint

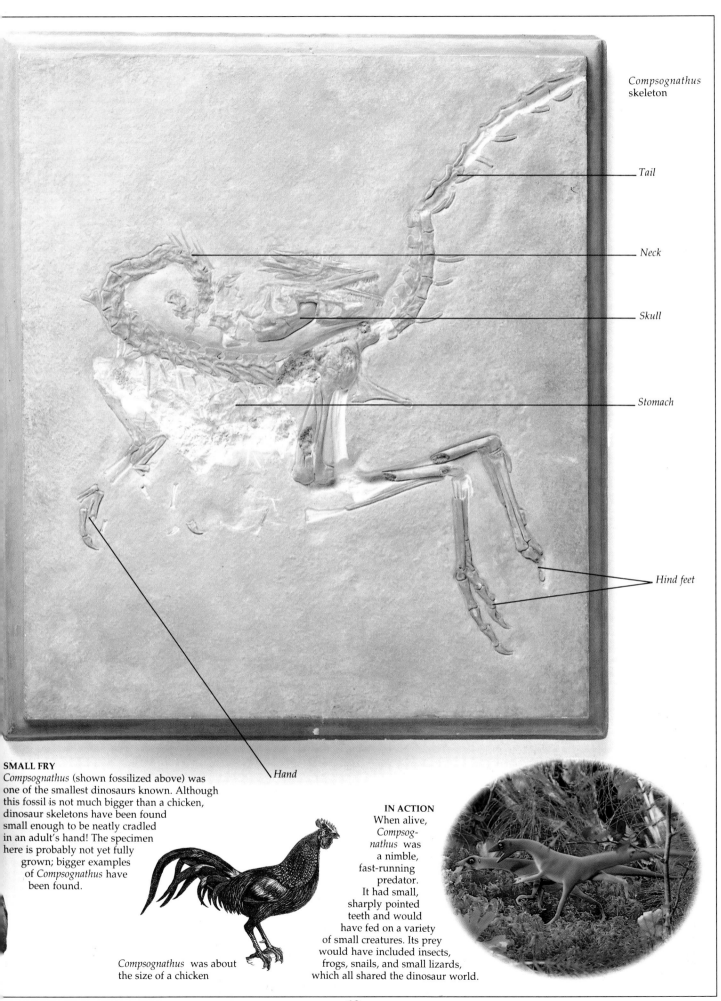

Compsognathus
skeleton

Tail

Neck

Skull

Stomach

Hind feet

Hand

SMALL FRY
Compsognathus (shown fossilized above) was
one of the smallest dinosaurs known. Although
this fossil is not much bigger than a chicken,
dinosaur skeletons have been found
small enough to be neatly cradled
in an adult's hand! The specimen
here is probably not yet fully
grown; bigger examples
of *Compsognathus* have
been found.

IN ACTION
When alive,
*Compsog-
nathus* was
a nimble,
fast-running
predator.
It had small,
sharply pointed
teeth and would
have fed on a variety
of small creatures. Its prey
would have included insects,
frogs, snails, and small lizards,
which all shared the dinosaur world.

Compsognathus was about
the size of a chicken

The long-necked beast

THE MASSIVE CREATURE that can be seen spread across the next eight pages was one of the biggest dinosaurs ever to walk the Earth. It was called *Diplodocus*, and like *Mamenchisaurus*, opposite, it belonged to a group of dinosaurs called sauropods (p. 12). *Diplodocus* looked extraordinary with its long neck and tail, and a head that was tiny in proportion to the rest of its body. This type of body suited its lifestyle perfectly. It could reach up to feed at the tops of the very tall trees, like conifers (evergreens), that grew at the time. Its small head allowed it to graze on vegetation that few other dinosaurs could reach. This type of feeding needed a special type of neck - one that was strong, light, and flexible, in order to be raised and lowered easily. Having stripped one area bare of food, it would have strolled off with its companions in search of new feeding grounds. If *Diplodocus* was threatened by a meat eater, its only defense would have been its bulk and its long, whiplike tail (pp. 20-21).

Small skull compared to size of body

MAN AND BEAST
When a man is shown next to the skeleton, the enormous size of *Diplodocus* can be appreciated. *Diplodocus* was 86 ft (26 m) long, and its great weight (15 tons) was supported by huge straight legs, like pillars.

Cycad plant would have formed part of Diplodocus' *diet*

SHORT AND FLEXIBLE
Unlike *Diplodocus*, a predator such as *Tyrannosaurus rex* (left) needed a neck that was short, powerful, and flexible. It had to be short to support the large head. Flexibility in the neck meant that *Tyrannosaurus rex* could twist its head around to wrench flesh from its prey.

A GIRAFFE'S LIFE
Like *Diplodocus*, giraffes reach into the treetops with their long necks. But unlike the dinosaur, the giraffe has grinding teeth and can chew its food so it does not need such a large belly.

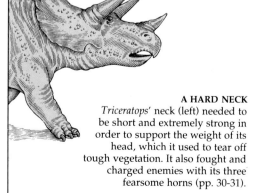

A HARD NECK
Triceratops' neck (left) needed to be short and extremely strong in order to support the weight of its head, which it used to tear off tough vegetation. It also fought and charged enemies with its three fearsome horns (pp. 30-31).

DIPLODOCUS AT HOME
Diplodocus is often shown living in marshy land, but this habitat would not have suited it at all. Because it had narrow feet in proportion to its body weight (like an elephant's), it probably would have sunk into the mud and got stuck. It would have preferred a landscape like this one - dry, with firm ground, where it would browse its way through conifer forests, perhaps as part of a herd.

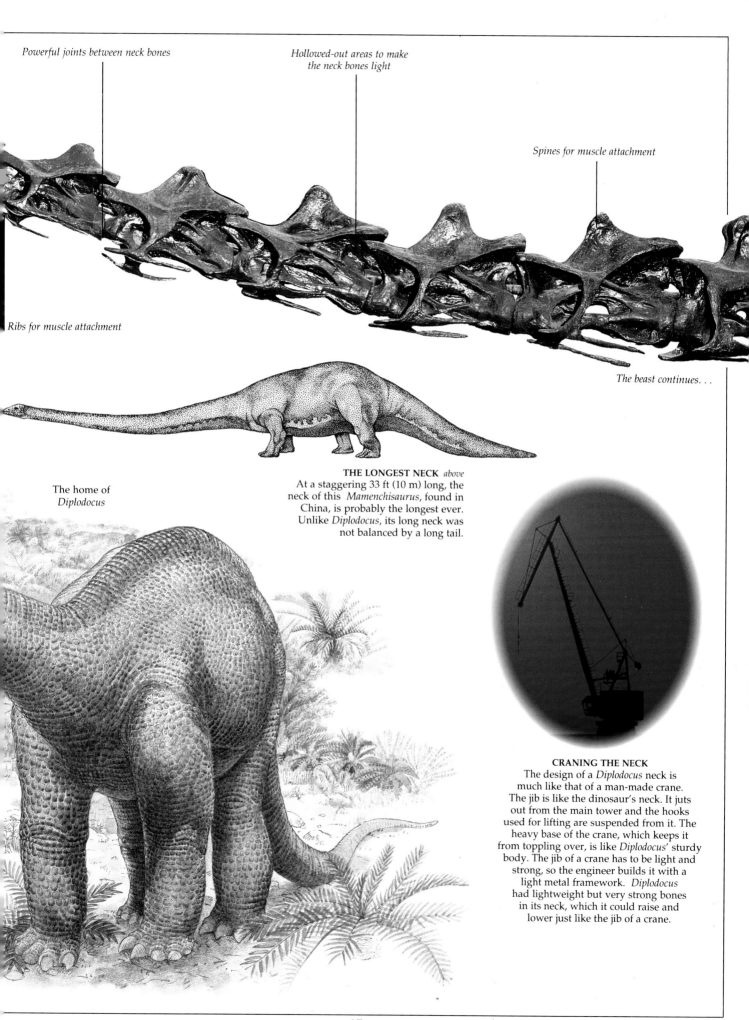

Powerful joints between neck bones

Hollowed-out areas to make
the neck bones light

Spines for muscle attachment

Ribs for muscle attachment

The beast continues. . .

The home of
Diplodocus

THE LONGEST NECK *above*
At a staggering 33 ft (10 m) long, the
neck of this *Mamenchisaurus*, found in
China, is probably the longest ever.
Unlike *Diplodocus*, its long neck was
not balanced by a long tail.

CRANING THE NECK
The design of a *Diplodocus* neck is
much like that of a man-made crane.
The jib is like the dinosaur's neck. It juts
out from the main tower and the hooks
used for lifting are suspended from it. The
heavy base of the crane, which keeps it
from toppling over, is like *Diplodocus'* sturdy
body. The jib of a crane has to be light and
strong, so the engineer builds it with a
light metal framework. *Diplodocus*
had lightweight but very strong bones
in its neck, which it could raise and
lower just like the jib of a crane.

Neck bone

Scapula
(shoulder blade)

The backbone story

The body of *Diplodocus* was designed to bear and move enormous weight, and the backbone, between shoulders and hips, was the powerhouse of the whole animal. The back bones (vertebrae) had to be strong enough to support the enormous weight of the neck, tail, and belly. However, they were hollowed out for lightness. Narrow spines, pointing upward from the top of the backbone, acted as anchor points for powerful back muscles. Long ribs pointing downward curved around the belly and helped to hold the backbone in position against the great weight of the belly. They also protected the internal organs of the animal.

Humerus
(upper arm bone)

Ulna
(forearm bone)

Temple of Jupiter, Athens

Radius
(forearm bone)

Wrist

LEGS LIKE PILLARS
The strong legs of *Diplodocus* supported its body just as the pillars of this Greek temple support the heavy stone roof. The limb bones were heavy and dense, capable of holding up the enormous weight of the dinosaur's body.

Hand

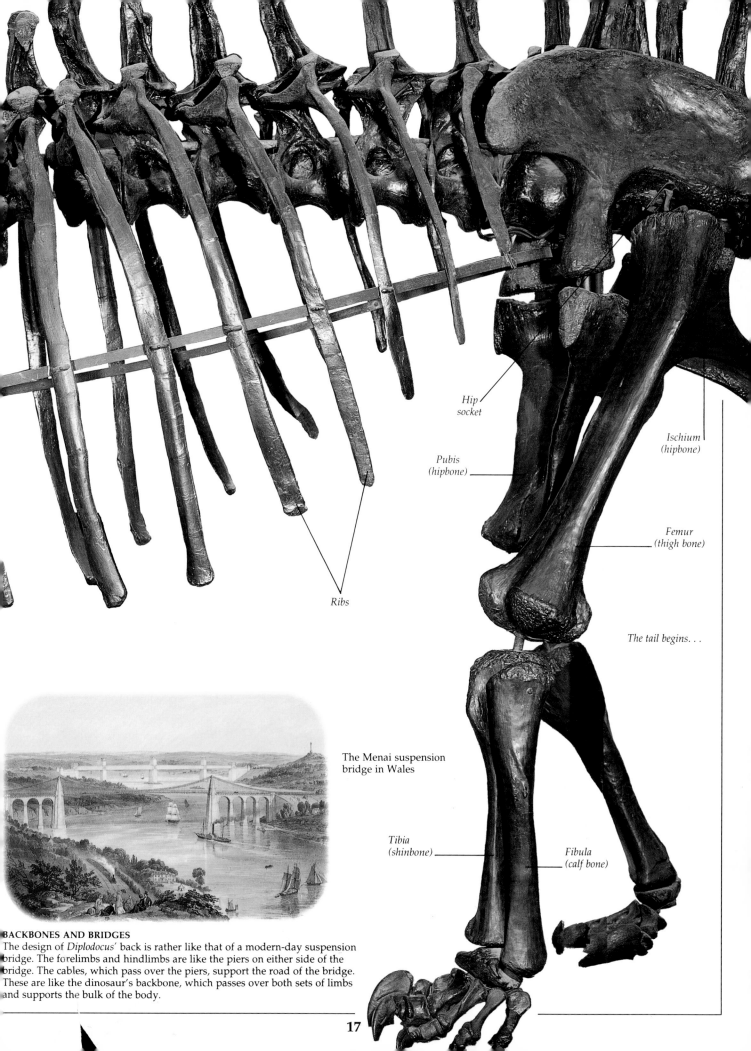

Hip
socket

Ischium
(hipbone)

Pubis
(hipbone)

Femur
(thigh bone)

The tail begins. . .

Ribs

The Menai suspension
bridge in Wales

Tibia
(shinbone)

Fibula
(calf bone)

BACKBONES AND BRIDGES

The design of *Diplodocus'* back is rather like that of a modern-day suspension
bridge. The forelimbs and hindlimbs are like the piers on either side of the
bridge. The cables, which pass over the piers, support the road of the bridge.
These are like the dinosaur's backbone, which passes over both sets of limbs
and supports the bulk of the body.

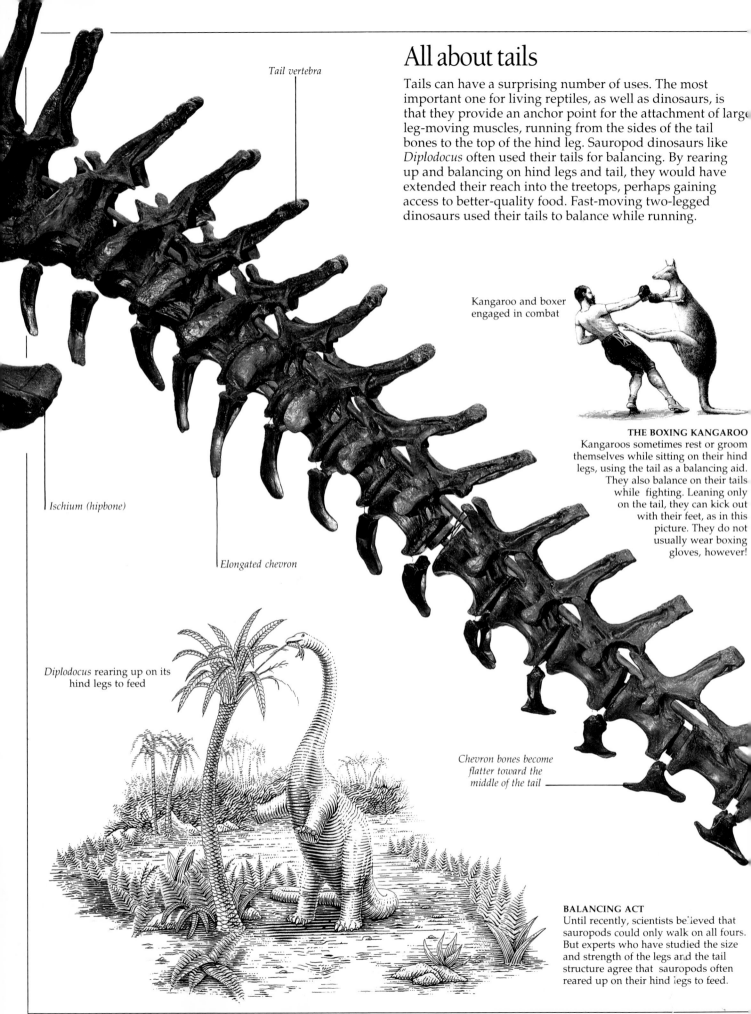

All about tails

Tails can have a surprising number of uses. The most important one for living reptiles, as well as dinosaurs, is that they provide an anchor point for the attachment of large leg-moving muscles, running from the sides of the tail bones to the top of the hind leg. Sauropod dinosaurs like *Diplodocus* often used their tails for balancing. By rearing up and balancing on hind legs and tail, they would have extended their reach into the treetops, perhaps gaining access to better-quality food. Fast-moving two-legged dinosaurs used their tails to balance while running.

Tail vertebra

Ischium (hipbone)

Elongated chevron

Kangaroo and boxer engaged in combat

THE BOXING KANGAROO
Kangaroos sometimes rest or groom themselves while sitting on their hind legs, using the tail as a balancing aid. They also balance on their tails while fighting. Leaning only on the tail, they can kick out with their feet, as in this picture. They do not usually wear boxing gloves, however!

Diplodocus rearing up on its hind legs to feed

Chevron bones become flatter toward the middle of the tail

BALANCING ACT
Until recently, scientists believed that sauropods could only walk on all fours. But experts who have studied the size and strength of the legs and the tail structure agree that sauropods often reared up on their hind legs to feed.

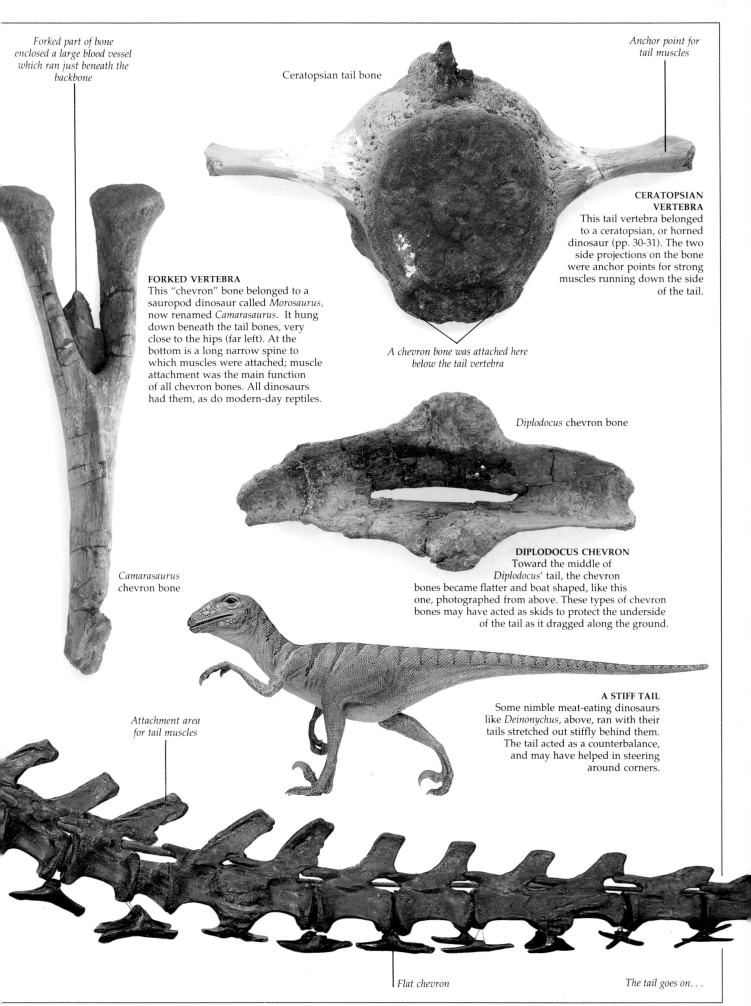

Forked part of bone enclosed a large blood vessel which ran just beneath the backbone

Ceratopsian tail bone

Anchor point for tail muscles

CERATOPSIAN VERTEBRA
This tail vertebra belonged to a ceratopsian, or horned dinosaur (pp. 30-31). The two side projections on the bone were anchor points for strong muscles running down the side of the tail.

FORKED VERTEBRA
This "chevron" bone belonged to a sauropod dinosaur called *Morosaurus*, now renamed *Camarasaurus*. It hung down beneath the tail bones, very close to the hips (far left). At the bottom is a long narrow spine to which muscles were attached; muscle attachment was the main function of all chevron bones. All dinosaurs had them, as do modern-day reptiles.

A chevron bone was attached here below the tail vertebra

Diplodocus chevron bone

Camarasaurus chevron bone

DIPLODOCUS CHEVRON
Toward the middle of *Diplodocus*' tail, the chevron bones became flatter and boat shaped, like this one, photographed from above. These types of chevron bones may have acted as skids to protect the underside of the tail as it dragged along the ground.

Attachment area for tail muscles

A STIFF TAIL
Some nimble meat-eating dinosaurs like *Deinonychus*, above, ran with their tails stretched out stiffly behind them. The tail acted as a counterbalance, and may have helped in steering around corners.

Flat chevron

The tail goes on. . .

19

The tale of defense

TAILS WERE A VERY USEFUL MEANS of defense for many plant-eating dinosaurs - what they lacked in teeth and claws they made up for with their ingenious tails. Some dinosaurs, like the sauropods, had long, thin tails which they used like whips. This was their main form of defense. Armored dinosaurs, or ankylosaurs, wielded bony clubs on their tails. Stegosaurs, or plated dinosaurs (pp. 34-35), had sharp, fearsome tail spikes which they used to lash out at attackers. Some modern-day reptiles use their tails in self-defense: crocodiles will lash out at an enemy with their heavy, scale-covered tails, and many lizards have long whiplike tails. No living reptiles, however, have tails with attachments as spectacular as the formidable spikes and clubs used by some dinosaurs to defend themselves.

A SEVERE BLOW
Shown here delivering a crippling blow to a tyrannosaur is the armored dinosaur *Euoplocephalus*. Although no match for the meat eater in size, *Euoplocephalus* could topple and disable the tyrannosaur with one well-aimed blow of its tail club.

THORNY DEVIL
Some living reptiles, like this Moloch lizard, are so well armored from head to toe that they don't need a special defensive tail. Few predators would attempt an attack on this spiked lizard. It lives in dry or desert areas of Australia.

Bony studs

Long muscular tail

Scelidosaurus

USEFUL TAIL
Scelidosaurus was a plant eater that relied mostly on its armored skin to protect it from predators. But its long tail may have given it an extra advantage. It could have used the tail to help balance on its hind legs while running away from a predator.

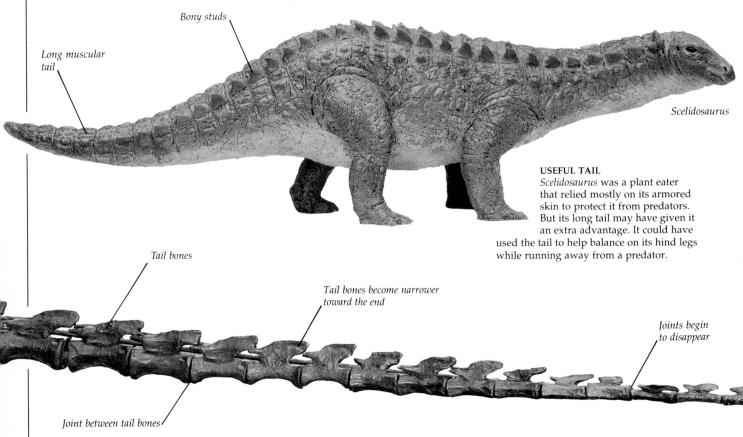

Tail bones

Tail bones become narrower toward the end

Joints begin to disappear

Joint between tail bones

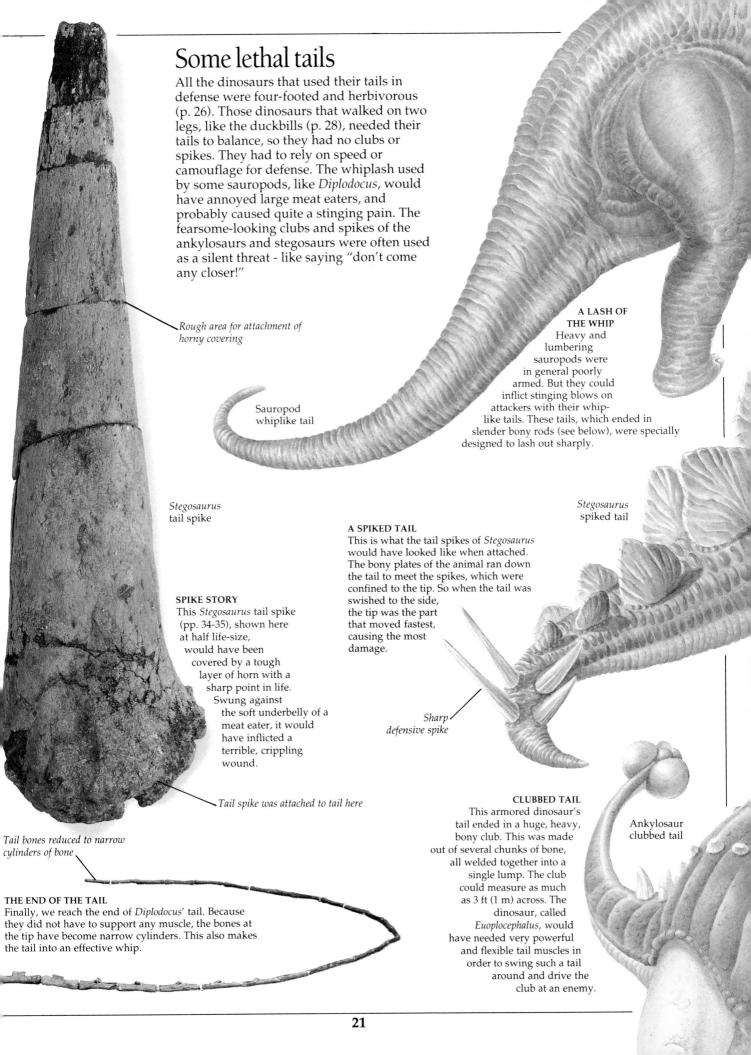

Some lethal tails

All the dinosaurs that used their tails in defense were four-footed and herbivorous (p. 26). Those dinosaurs that walked on two legs, like the duckbills (p. 28), needed their tails to balance, so they had no clubs or spikes. They had to rely on speed or camouflage for defense. The whiplash used by some sauropods, like *Diplodocus*, would have annoyed large meat eaters, and probably caused quite a stinging pain. The fearsome-looking clubs and spikes of the ankylosaurs and stegosaurs were often used as a silent threat - like saying "don't come any closer!"

Rough area for attachment of horny covering

Sauropod whiplike tail

Stegosaurus tail spike

Stegosaurus spiked tail

A LASH OF THE WHIP
Heavy and lumbering sauropods were in general poorly armed. But they could inflict stinging blows on attackers with their whip-like tails. These tails, which ended in slender bony rods (see below), were specially designed to lash out sharply.

A SPIKED TAIL
This is what the tail spikes of *Stegosaurus* would have looked like when attached. The bony plates of the animal ran down the tail to meet the spikes, which were confined to the tip. So when the tail was swished to the side, the tip was the part that moved fastest, causing the most damage.

SPIKE STORY
This *Stegosaurus* tail spike (pp. 34-35), shown here at half life-size, would have been covered by a tough layer of horn with a sharp point in life. Swung against the soft underbelly of a meat eater, it would have inflicted a terrible, crippling wound.

Sharp defensive spike

Tail spike was attached to tail here

Tail bones reduced to narrow cylinders of bone

THE END OF THE TAIL
Finally, we reach the end of *Diplodocus'* tail. Because they did not have to support any muscle, the bones at the tip have become narrow cylinders. This also makes the tail into an effective whip.

CLUBBED TAIL
This armored dinosaur's tail ended in a huge, heavy, bony club. This was made out of several chunks of bone, all welded together into a single lump. The club could measure as much as 3 ft (1 m) across. The dinosaur, called *Euoplocephalus*, would have needed very powerful and flexible tail muscles in order to swing such a tail around and drive the club at an enemy.

Ankylosaur clubbed tail

Dinosaur diets

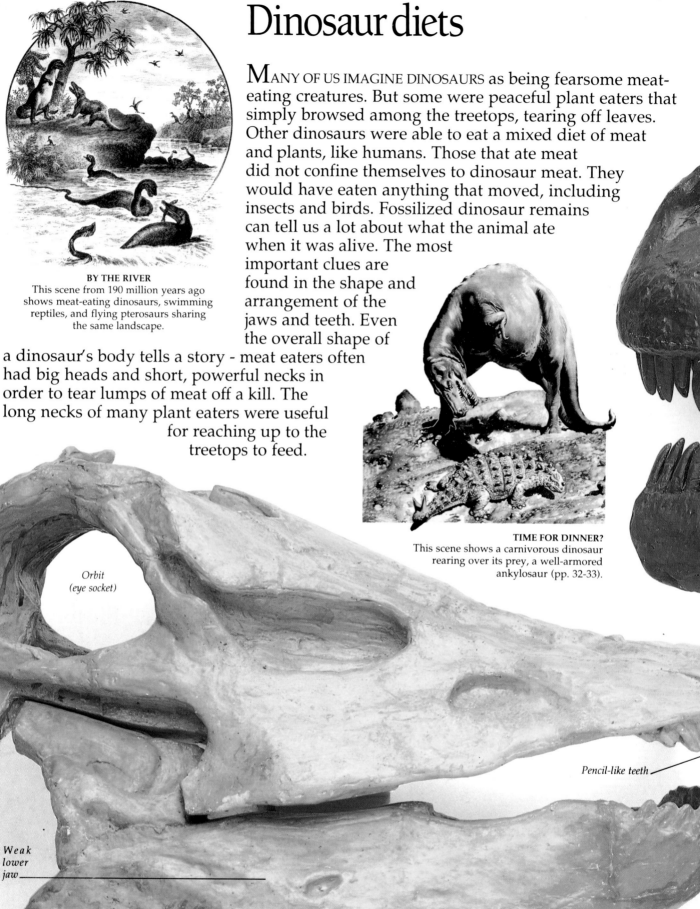

Many of us imagine dinosaurs as being fearsome meat-eating creatures. But some were peaceful plant eaters that simply browsed among the treetops, tearing off leaves. Other dinosaurs were able to eat a mixed diet of meat and plants, like humans. Those that ate meat did not confine themselves to dinosaur meat. They would have eaten anything that moved, including insects and birds. Fossilized dinosaur remains can tell us a lot about what the animal ate when it was alive. The most important clues are found in the shape and arrangement of the jaws and teeth. Even the overall shape of a dinosaur's body tells a story - meat eaters often had big heads and short, powerful necks in order to tear lumps of meat off a kill. The long necks of many plant eaters were useful for reaching up to the treetops to feed.

BY THE RIVER
This scene from 190 million years ago shows meat-eating dinosaurs, swimming reptiles, and flying pterosaurs sharing the same landscape.

TIME FOR DINNER?
This scene shows a carnivorous dinosaur rearing over its prey, a well-armored ankylosaur (pp. 32-33).

Orbit
(eye socket)

Pencil-like teeth

Weak
lower
jaw

Diplodocus skull

SERIOUS TEETH

The fearsome rows of curved, serrated (sawlike) teeth in the *Allosaurus* skull (below) are typical of carnivores (meat eaters). The "windows" in the massive skull helped to reduce its weight. *Allosaurus* may have fed on the young of herbivores such as *Diplodocus* (opposite). An adult *Diplodocus* would have been too big to tackle, unless *Allosaurus* hunted in packs.

Large cavity in front of eye for jaw muscles

Orbit (eye socket)

Large serrated teeth

Allosaurus skull

VEGETARIAN SKULL *left*

This skull belonged to a huge plant eater, or herbivore, called *Diplodocus*. All of the thin, pencil-like teeth are at the front of the mouth. *Diplodocus* would have used them like a rake to draw in pine needles and leaves. Unable to chew, *Diplodocus* simply swallowed what it raked in.

Powerful lower jaw

Diplodocus

DIPLODOCUS DINNER

Diplodocus may have raked in plants like this fern leaf. Because it never chewed, it did not need a strong lower jaw.

Orbit (eye socket)

Massospondylus skull (below)

Small coarse teeth

DUAL-DIET DINOSAUR

The skull above belonged to a *Massospondylus*. Its small, coarse-edged teeth were multi-purpose - they could chew either meat or plants. Animals who can eat like this are called omnivores.

23

Meat eaters

ALL THE MEAT-EATING DINOSAURS belonged to a group called Theropoda, which means "beast footed." Some of the meat-eating dinosaurs were called carnosaurs or "flesh lizards" - large animals with big heads, powerful legs, and short arms. Like all theropods, they walked on two legs, probably not very fast because of the bulk they had to carry. They had big heads which held long jaws lined with huge curved teeth, serrated like steak knives. Carnosaurs pursued and ate other dinosaurs, and also fed on dead animals that they found. They would kill their prey with the help of their clawed feet and then tear off the flesh of the victim with their hands and teeth. Their hands were also well-equipped with sharp claws. The other meat eaters were known as coelurosaurs, or "hollow-tailed lizards." Coelurosaurs were lightly built, nimble creatures with long grasping arms and hands and long, narrow jaws. They could run very fast and could catch small mammals and insects. After a carnosaur had eaten its fill, a coelurosaur would often move in to eat the leftover scraps.

SMALL BUT VICIOUS
It is hard to believe that a dinosaur tooth (left) could be smaller than a human incisor, or cutting tooth (right). This dinosaur tooth belonged to *Troödon*, or "wounding tooth."

The king

Tyrannosaurus rex is probably the best known (and most fearsome) of the carnosaurs. It was 49 ft (15 m) long and had a massive skull with powerful jaws that held serrated teeth up to 7 in (18 cm) long. It probably used its tiny arms to push itself upright after it had been lying down.

Backward-curving teeth gave carnosaurs a better grip on a victim

Albertosaurus lower jaw

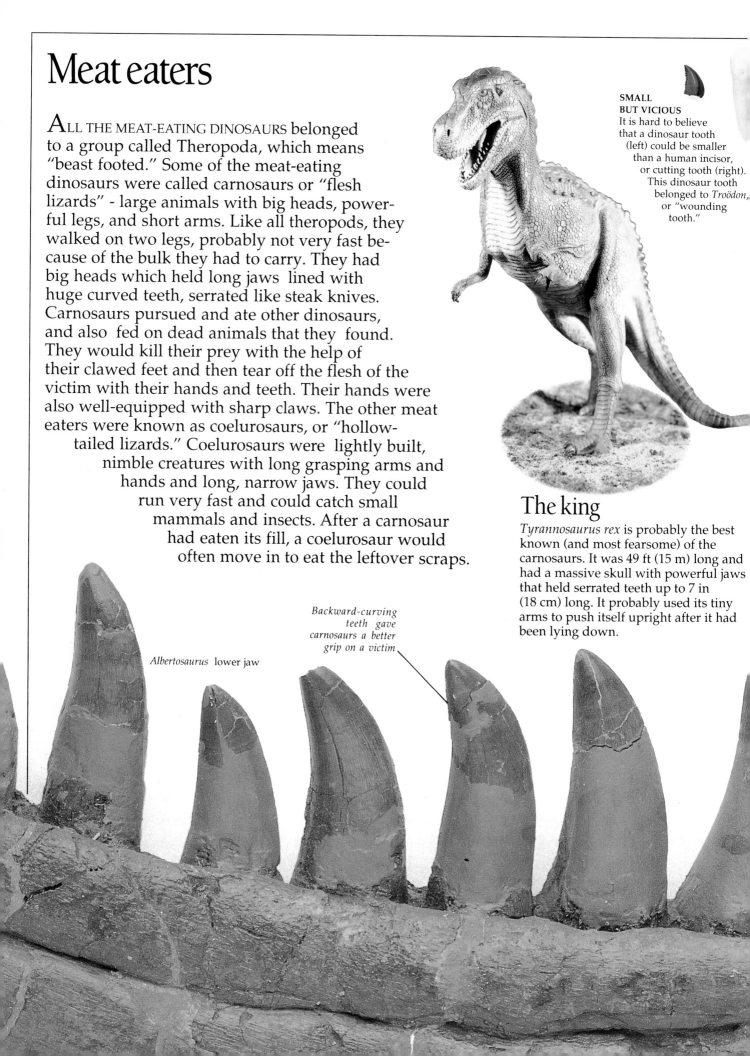

NUTHETES TOOTH
Still embedded in rock, this tooth came from a small meat eater called *Nuthetes*.

SMALLER GNASHER
Not all tyrannosaur teeth were huge. This small one is curved, in order to hook into its victim.

LION'S SLICER
Meat-eating animals, like lions, have developed special slicing teeth. No dinosaur had a tooth like this.

NEW GNASHER
Meat-eating dinosaurs' teeth kept growing and were constantly replaced throughout life. This megalosaur tooth is a "new" one.

The large, curved tooth of *Megalosaurus*

Fine serrations like those on a steak knife

Cracks which occurred during fossilization

A LOSING BATTLE?
A 19th-century etching shows *Iguanodon* (left) and *Megalosaurus* (right) fighting each other. Although *Iguanodon* has been given sharp teeth by the artist, it was in fact a plant eater and would not have stood much chance against the strength of *Megalosaurus*. The spike on its nose was really on its thumb in life, and was its only real weapon of defense (pp. 8-9).

THE BIGGEST. . .
This large *Megalosaurus* tooth is of a typical carnosaur shape, with its curved edge pointing backward. The edges of the tooth are sharp, with sawlike serrations for cutting meat. The cracks on this specimen appeared during fossilization.

Ceratosaurus skull (below)

Sharp serrated front edge of tooth

Bony tooth socket

Inner side of jaw bone

LETHAL JAWBONE
This *Albertosaurus* lower jaw (left) stretched the length of the animal's skull. Powerful jaw muscles, reaching up behind the eye, were attached to the area without teeth. These would have produced a powerful bite, snapping the jaw shut on impact with its prey. The skull above, which belonged to another carnosaur, shows the same basic design.

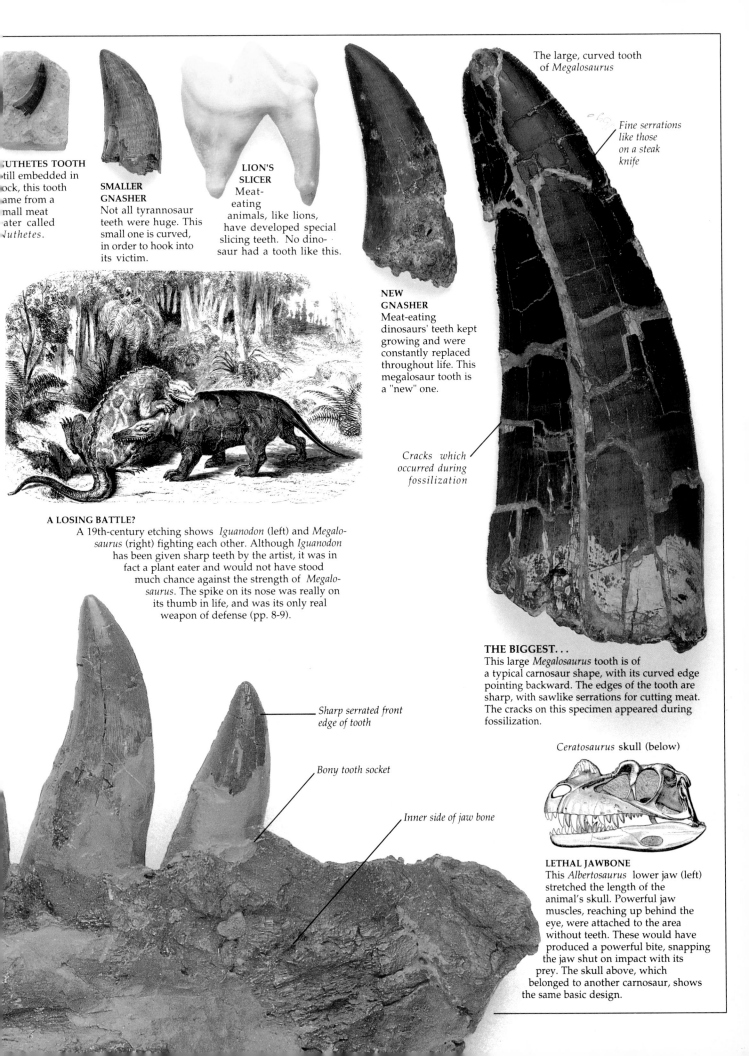

Plant eaters

MANY OF THE DINOSAURS were plant eaters, including the biggest of all, the sauropods (pp. 12-13). Eating a diet of plants causes animals many more problems than eating meat. Plants are made of tough materials like cellulose and woody lignin and need to be broken down before digestion can take place in the animal's stomach. Plant-eating dinosaurs coped with their diet in a variety of ways: the sauropods did not chew at all, but simply swallowed raked-in vegetation. This passed directly to the stomach and was ground up by deliberately swallowed gastroliths, or "gizzard stones," or was fermented by bacteria, as in a cow's stomach. The hadrosaurs, or duckbilled dinosaurs, had special teeth which ground and chopped their food before they swallowed it. Ceratopsians tackled tough plants with their extra-strong jaws and scissor-like teeth. All of the bird-hipped dinosaurs (p. 6) were plant eaters.

Plant-eating dinosaurs would have eaten evergreens such as this yew leaf

TINY TEETH
This jaw came from *Echinodon*, one of the smallest plant-eating dinosaurs. The tiny teeth had spiked edges, like those of an iguana lizard, which eats a mixed diet of plants and meat.

Main jawbone

Ceratopsian beak

SCISSOR TOOTH
This tooth came from a ceratopsian dinosaur, like *Triceratops* (below). After tearing off the vegetation with its beak (far left), it would then have sliced it up with its sharp teeth.

Notch for replacement tooth to grow into

Cycad plant

TOUGH AND STRINGY
Some experts believe that ceratopsian dinosaurs evolved specially enabling them to eat new kinds of tough plants. They would have eaten the leaves of palmlike cycads (left), and maybe even tackled pine cones (above).

Pine cone

BUILT TO CHEW
Dinosaurs like this *Triceratops* (pp. 30-31) ate tough, fibrous plants (above). *Triceratops*, like many ceratopsians, had extremely powerful jaws and sharp teeth that helped it tear out and eat these plants.

CROPPING BEAK
A beak like this ceratopsian one (p. 30) was ideal for cropping tough plants. The rough grooves and pits mark the place where the horny covering of keratin was attached. The lower, wider part of the bone (called the predentary) fitted tightly against the lower jaw.

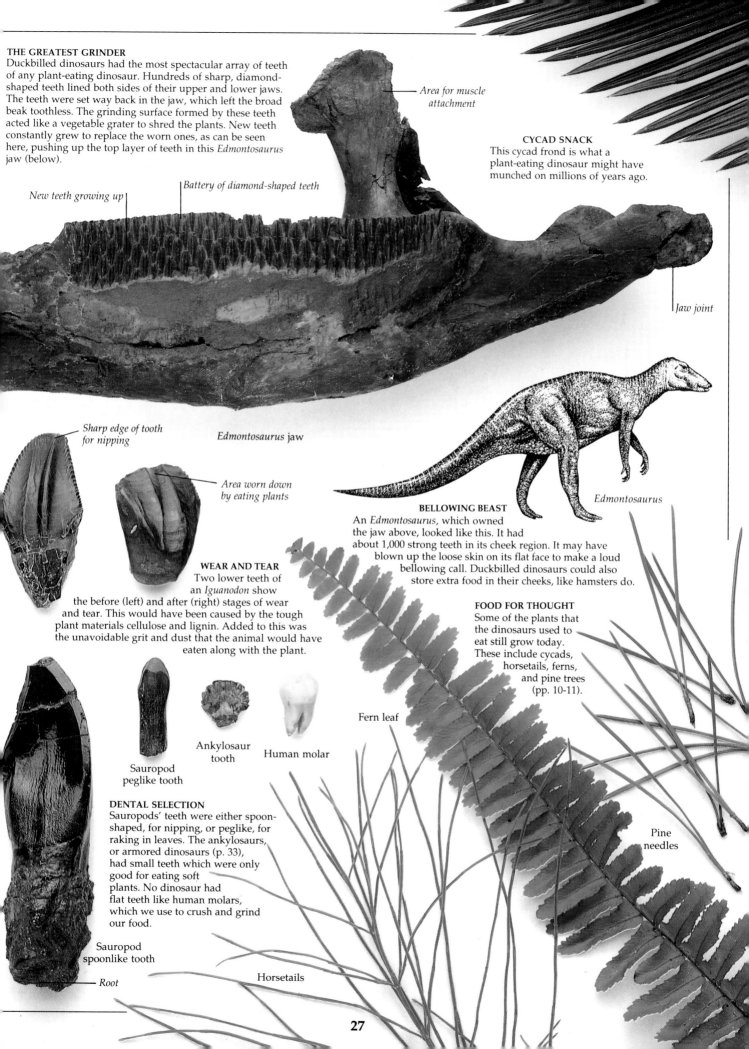

THE GREATEST GRINDER
Duckbilled dinosaurs had the most spectacular array of teeth of any plant-eating dinosaur. Hundreds of sharp, diamond-shaped teeth lined both sides of their upper and lower jaws. The teeth were set way back in the jaw, which left the broad beak toothless. The grinding surface formed by these teeth acted like a vegetable grater to shred the plants. New teeth constantly grew to replace the worn ones, as can be seen here, pushing up the top layer of teeth in this *Edmontosaurus* jaw (below).

Area for muscle attachment

CYCAD SNACK
This cycad frond is what a plant-eating dinosaur might have munched on millions of years ago.

New teeth growing up

Battery of diamond-shaped teeth

Jaw joint

Sharp edge of tooth for nipping

Edmontosaurus jaw

Area worn down by eating plants

Edmontosaurus

WEAR AND TEAR
Two lower teeth of an *Iguanodon* show the before (left) and after (right) stages of wear and tear. This would have been caused by the tough plant materials cellulose and lignin. Added to this was the unavoidable grit and dust that the animal would have eaten along with the plant.

BELLOWING BEAST
An *Edmontosaurus*, which owned the jaw above, looked like this. It had about 1,000 strong teeth in its cheek region. It may have blown up the loose skin on its flat face to make a loud bellowing call. Duckbilled dinosaurs could also store extra food in their cheeks, like hamsters do.

FOOD FOR THOUGHT
Some of the plants that the dinosaurs used to eat still grow today. These include cycads, horsetails, ferns, and pine trees (pp. 10-11).

Fern leaf

Sauropod peglike tooth

Ankylosaur tooth

Human molar

Pine needles

DENTAL SELECTION
Sauropods' teeth were either spoon-shaped, for nipping, or peglike, for raking in leaves. The ankylosaurs, or armored dinosaurs (p. 33), had small teeth which were only good for eating soft plants. No dinosaur had flat teeth like human molars, which we use to crush and grind our food.

Sauropod spoonlike tooth

Root

Horsetails

27

Peculiar heads

SOME DINOSAURS HAD very odd shaped heads, sprouting weird and wonderful projections of bone including lumps, bumps, crests, spikes, and helmets. These odd shapes were eyecatching and were probably used to attract a mate or scare away an enemy, just like the strange shapes and bright colors on some of today's reptiles, birds, and mammals. Dinosaurs with odd-shaped heads used them to defend or attack - a bony head could act like a natural safety helmet or a head-butting device. The most spectacular heads belonged to a group of dinosaurs called the hadrosaurs, or duckbills, so-called because of their broad, toothless beaks.

CREST FALLEN?
Different hadrosaurs had different head shapes, but their bodies were all quite similar. Some had heads with no projections at all, like this one, *Anatosaurus*, one of the most common "crestless" types. It used its broad ducklike beak to scoop up leaves.

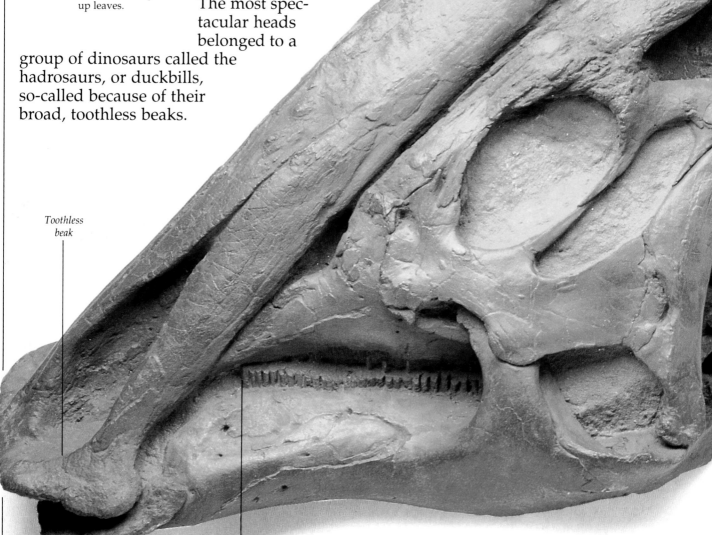

HEAD-CASE
The first two heads in this selection are duckbills: *Parasaurolophus*, with its distinctive long horn, and *Corythosaurus*, with its "dinner plate" shaped crest. The broad, thick head on the right belongs to *Pachycephalosaurus*, one of the "boneheaded" dinosaurs.

Toothless beak

Teeth start here

Parasaurolophus skull

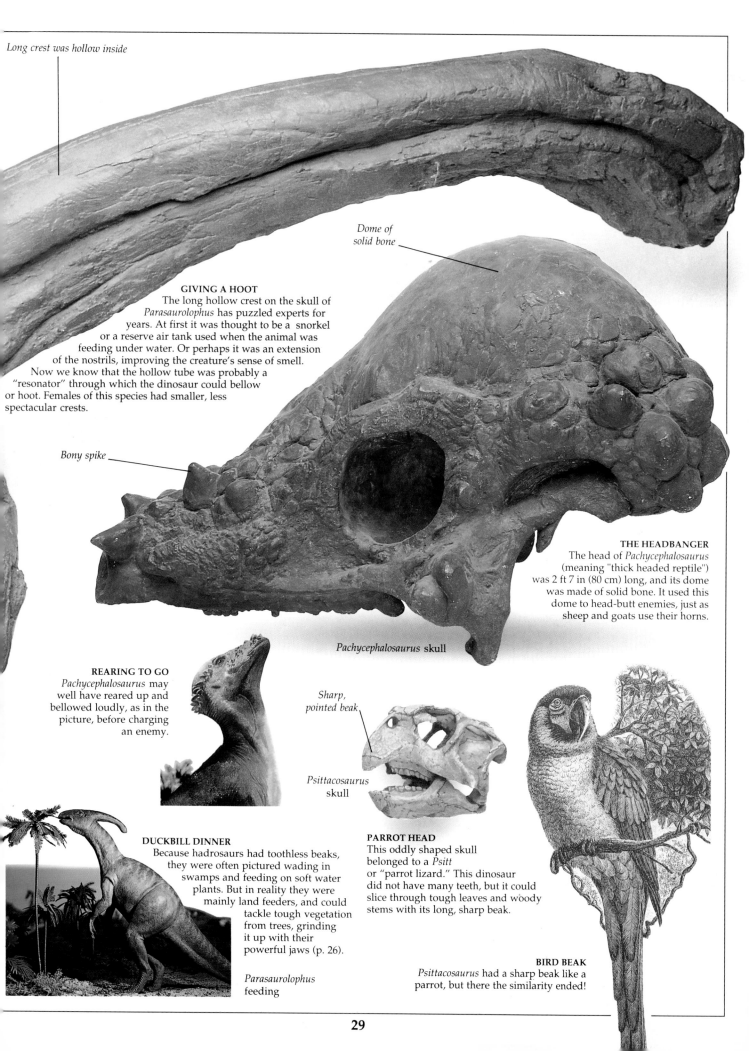

Long crest was hollow inside

Dome of solid bone

GIVING A HOOT
The long hollow crest on the skull of
Parasaurolophus has puzzled experts for
years. At first it was thought to be a snorkel
or a reserve air tank used when the animal was
feeding under water. Or perhaps it was an extension
of the nostrils, improving the creature's sense of smell.
Now we know that the hollow tube was probably a
"resonator" through which the dinosaur could bellow
or hoot. Females of this species had smaller, less
spectacular crests.

Bony spike

THE HEADBANGER
The head of *Pachycephalosaurus*
(meaning "thick headed reptile")
was 2 ft 7 in (80 cm) long, and its dome
was made of solid bone. It used this
dome to head-butt enemies, just as
sheep and goats use their horns.

Pachycephalosaurus skull

REARING TO GO
Pachycephalosaurus may
well have reared up and
bellowed loudly, as in the
picture, before charging
an enemy.

*Sharp,
pointed beak*

*Psittacosaurus
skull*

DUCKBILL DINNER
Because hadrosaurs had toothless beaks,
they were often pictured wading in
swamps and feeding on soft water
plants. But in reality they were
mainly land feeders, and could
tackle tough vegetation
from trees, grinding
it up with their
powerful jaws (p. 26).

Parasaurolophus
feeding

PARROT HEAD
This oddly shaped skull
belonged to a *Psitt*
or "parrot lizard." This dinosaur
did not have many teeth, but it could
slice through tough leaves and woody
stems with its long, sharp beak.

BIRD BEAK
Psittacosaurus had a sharp beak like a
parrot, but there the similarity ended!

29

Three-horned face

*T*RICERATOPS, WHICH MEANS "three-horned face," belonged to a group of dinosaurs known as ceratopsians, or horned dinosaurs. Each ceratopsian had a large bony frill pointing backward from the skull and masking the neck, horns on the nose or over the eyes, and a narrow, hooked beak. Most were four-legged and stocky, like the rhinoceroses of today, and all were plant eaters. Many fossils of ceratopsians found in the same area suggest that they roamed in herds, and faced threatening meat eaters as a pack. As the ceratopsians evolved, their headgear gradually became more spectacular. *Triceratops*, the "king" of the ceratopsians, lived at the end of the age of the dinosaurs, and had the most impressive array of horns and frills of all the ceratopsians: its head took up nearly one-third of its length. With head lowered and the horns pointing forward, all backed up by its enormous bulk, *Triceratops* must have been a tough challenge to predators such as *Tyrannosaurus rex* (p. 24).

Brow horn

LIKE A RHINO
This model reconstruction of *Triceratops*, based on the study of complete skeletons of the animal, is probably very close to life. Here, the resemblance to modern rhinoceroses is very striking.

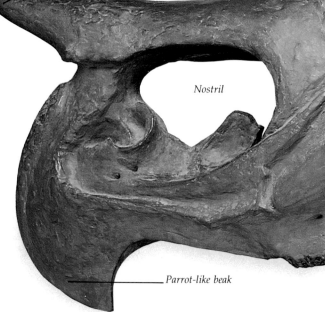

Nose horn

Nostril

Parrot-like beak

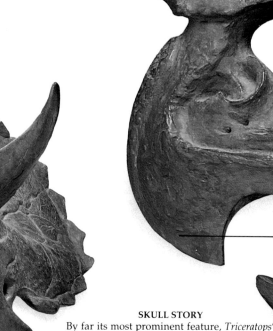

Wavy edge of frill

Triceratops
skull - front view

SKULL STORY
By far its most prominent feature, *Triceratops'* heavy skull can tell us a lot about its way of life. Its jaw was built to tackle very tough and fibrous plants. It snipped them off with its narrow, hooked beak and then sliced them up with its sharp, scissor-like teeth. The jaws were powered by huge muscles that extended up into the frill. The frill probably acted as an anchor for the jaw muscles, and also protected the neck. *Triceratops* used its sharp horns mainly for defense against tyrannosaurs, but it also used them in one-to-one combat. The male *Triceratops* would lock horns with a member of its own kind and head-wrestle, much as deer, antelope, and sheep do today.

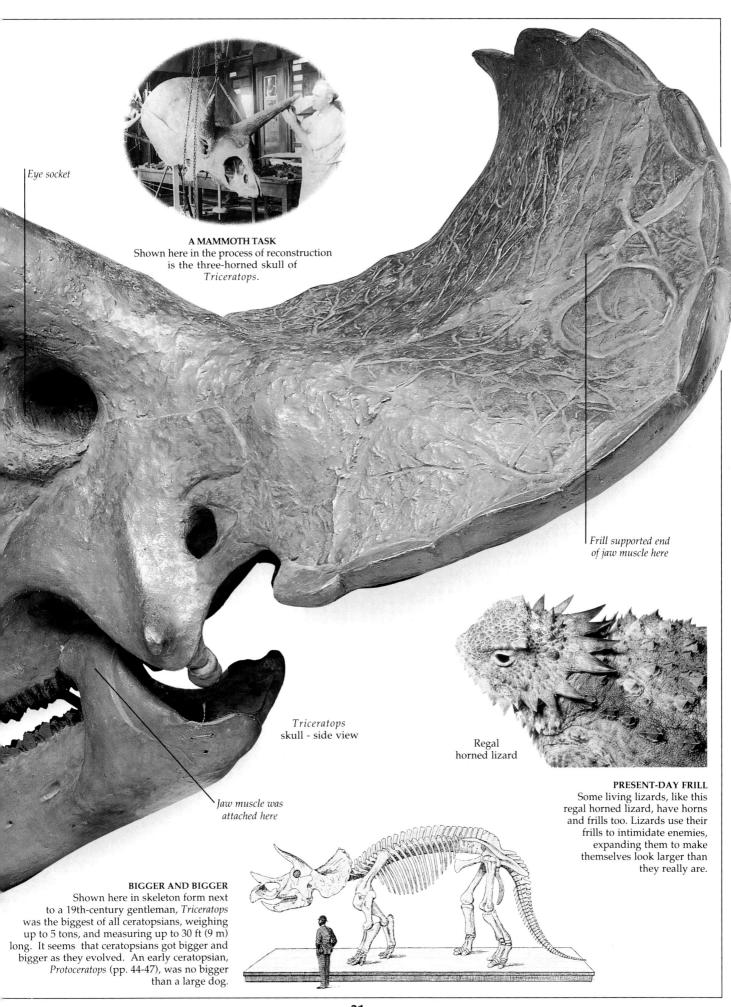

Eye socket

A MAMMOTH TASK
Shown here in the process of reconstruction
is the three-horned skull of
Triceratops.

*Frill supported end
of jaw muscle here*

Triceratops
skull - side view

*Jaw muscle was
attached here*

Regal
horned lizard

PRESENT-DAY FRILL
Some living lizards, like this
regal horned lizard, have horns
and frills too. Lizards use their
frills to intimidate enemies,
expanding them to make
themselves look larger than
they really are.

BIGGER AND BIGGER
Shown here in skeleton form next
to a 19th-century gentleman, *Triceratops*
was the biggest of all ceratopsians, weighing
up to 5 tons, and measuring up to 30 ft (9 m)
long. It seems that ceratopsians got bigger and
bigger as they evolved. An early ceratopsian,
Protoceratops (pp. 44-47), was no bigger
than a large dog.

A tough skin

W**HAT WAS** dinosaur skin like? Fossilized skin impressions can tell us that it was scaly, like reptile skin, and in some cases armor-plated for extra protection. Dinosaur skin was perfectly suited to life on land. Just like reptile skin, it was waterproof, tough, and horny. Waterproof skin prevents an animal from drying out quickly in air, sun, or wind - animals like frogs have to stay in moist conditions because their skin is thin and not waterproof. Tough, scaly skin protects an animal while it moves around on land, dragging its body over or between rough stones, or falling over. Dinosaur skin impressions, like the ones shown here, are usually small because after death, animal skin rots away too quickly to be fossilized. However, in a few rare cases, an almost entire body impression has been preserved. The dinosaurs that left these impressions probably died in a dry area so that their skin dried out before they were buried by windblown sand. The sand then turned into sandstone over the years, and was so tightly packed against the skin that when the skin disappeared, its exact shape and pattern remained in the stone. No one knows for sure what color dinosaur skin was, or whether it had stripes or spots - dinosaurs are most often shown in muddy shades of green and brown.

ARMOR-PLATED MAMMAL
Well protected by its bony armor, the armadillo that lives today is like the ankylosaurs, or armored dinosaurs (right). They, too, stayed still on the ground while predators were threatening. Few attackers would have been able to get a grip on their tough bodies.

COLOR COORDINATED
Dinosaurs may well have had brightly colored skin like this agamid lizard. Skin color can be useful as camouflage or as a warning signal. This lizard probably uses his bright-green skin to mark out a territory or to attract a mate.

SOLITARY NODULE
Bony nodules like this one were mixed in with the overlapping plates on *Polacanthus* skin. These nodules "floated" in the skin beneath the scales, as in living reptiles.

Polacanthus skin impression

A KNOBBY COAT
This knobby skin impression came from an armored dinosaur called *Polacanthus*. Short-legged and squat, it was about 13 ft (4 m) long and had sharp spines running along its back. These, combined with its overlapping bony plates, would have discouraged hungry meat eaters from attacking.

Raised nodules for protection

LIKE A CROCODILE?
Crocodiles are reptiles and have the same type of skin as the dinosaurs - ideally adapted to conditions on dry land. The knobby skin on this "smiling" crocodile is like the *Polacanthus* impression (left).

Central ridge of nodule

ALL ABOUT ANKYLOSAURS

The ankylosaurs had bones which were fused together to form a bony armor. These squat and very heavy creatures were the armored tanks of the dinosaur world. They looked much like giant reptilian armadillos. They had small jaws and weak teeth, and ate plants. They protected themselves from large carnivores mainly by crouching and clinging to the ground, relying completely on their tough skin for defense.

THE COMPLETE BEAST

A typical ankylosaur probably looked like this when it was alive. As well as having spikes and nodules, some of these dinosaurs had huge tail clubs (pp. 20-21) which they swung at the legs of attackers.

Smaller scales for flexibility

ANKYLOSAUR NODULE

Many ankylosaur nodules looked like this one. The flattened base was attached to the creature's back, and the broad central ridge provided protection. In life, it was covered by a horny scale (like a fingernail). In the picture it is possible to make out the pitted areas where this was attached.

Sauropod skin impression

Bigger scales where skin did not have to bend

UNARMORED AND SCALY

This skin impression, smooth compared to the ankylosaurs', came from a sauropod dinosaur, probably one like *Diplodocus* (pp. 14-21). The skin was scaly, not bony like the ankylosaur's, and would have given little protection against attack. The scales, although packed tightly together, had flexible edges where they touched, which acted like hinges to allow easy movement. You can see from this impression that the scales varied in size, the smaller ones occurring where the skin had to bend a lot.

Plated dinosaurs

ONE OF THE MOST UNUSUAL GROUPS of dinosaurs was the stegosaurs, named after the North American dinosaur *Stegosaurus*. Easily recognized by the double row of plates running down their backs, stegosaurs also had sharp spikes on the ends of their tails, used for lashing out in defense. Despite their frightening appearance, these dinosaurs were all plant eaters. They usually walked on all fours, grazing on low vegetation - a way of feeding that suited their low-slung heads perfectly. Their small weak teeth could only handle soft plants. The word "stegosaur" actually means "roof lizard" - it was once thought that the plates lay flat on the dinosaur's back, like tiles on a roof. Although this arrangement would have provided slightly better protection against attack from carnosaurs, it is more likely that the plates stood upright in two rows along the stegosaur's back. Some people think that the plates were fixed to the skeleton, but actually they were embedded in the dinosaur's thick skin.

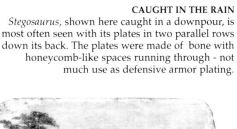

CAUGHT IN THE RAIN
Stegosaurus, shown here caught in a downpour, is most often seen with its plates in two parallel rows down its back. The plates were made of bone with honeycomb-like spaces running through - not much use as defensive armor plating.

A WEIRD STEGOSAUR
This etching shows an early attempt to reconstruct a plated dinosaur - with hedgehog-like spines instead of bony plates! It is unlikely that stegosaurs would have walked on two legs - their front feet were not adapted for any function except walking.

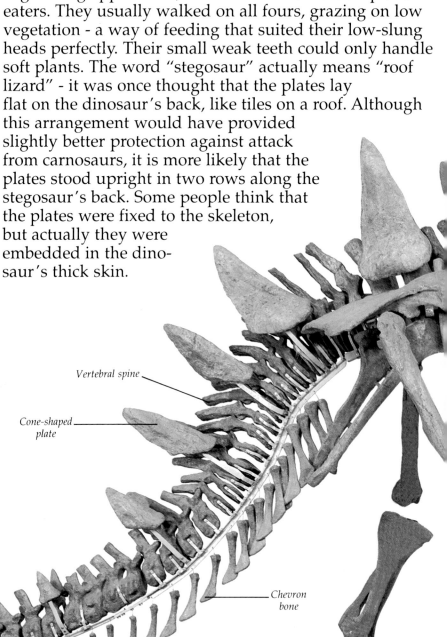

Vertebral spine

Cone-shaped plate

Chevron bone

A STING IN THE TAIL
The large, cone-shaped plates on the back of *Tuojiangosaurus* give way to two pairs of sharply pointed spikes, which were used as lethal weapons. Stegosaurs could swing their muscular tails from side to side with great force.

Sharp defensive spike

Broad, flat feet

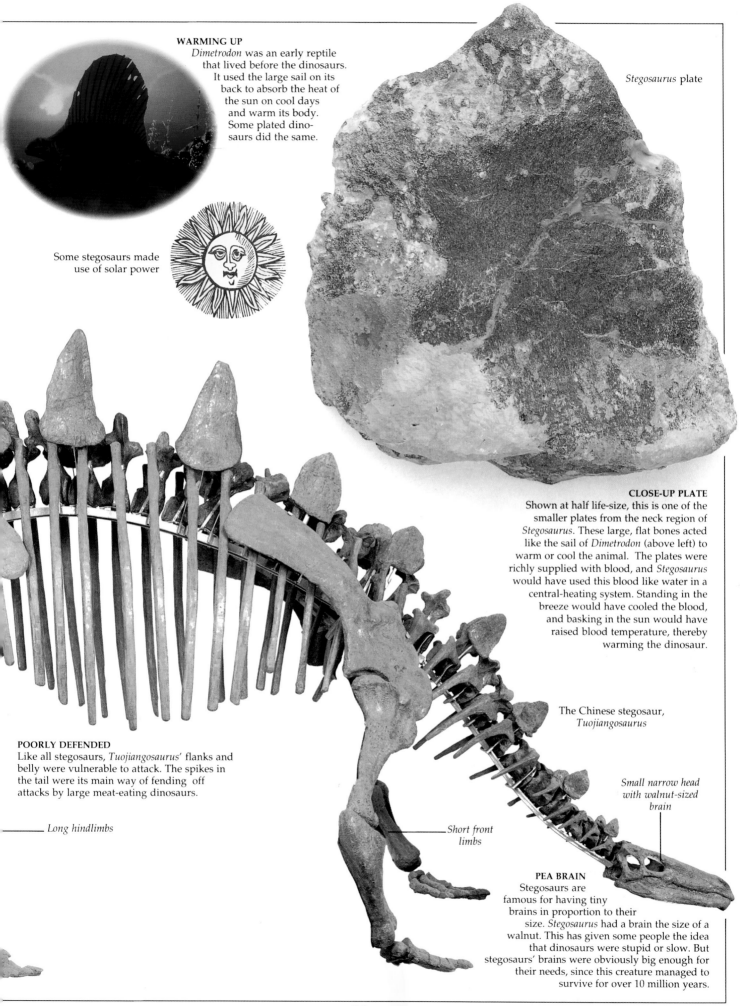

WARMING UP
Dimetrodon was an early reptile that lived before the dinosaurs. It used the large sail on its back to absorb the heat of the sun on cool days and warm its body. Some plated dinosaurs did the same.

Some stegosaurs made use of solar power

Stegosaurus plate

CLOSE-UP PLATE
Shown at half life-size, this is one of the smaller plates from the neck region of *Stegosaurus*. These large, flat bones acted like the sail of *Dimetrodon* (above left) to warm or cool the animal. The plates were richly supplied with blood, and *Stegosaurus* would have used this blood like water in a central-heating system. Standing in the breeze would have cooled the blood, and basking in the sun would have raised blood temperature, thereby warming the dinosaur.

The Chinese stegosaur, *Tuojiangosaurus*

Small narrow head with walnut-sized brain

POORLY DEFENDED
Like all stegosaurs, *Tuojiangosaurus'* flanks and belly were vulnerable to attack. The spikes in the tail were its main way of fending off attacks by large meat-eating dinosaurs.

_____ *Long hindlimbs*

Short front limbs

PEA BRAIN
Stegosaurs are famous for having tiny brains in proportion to their size. *Stegosaurus* had a brain the size of a walnut. This has given some people the idea that dinosaurs were stupid or slow. But stegosaurs' brains were obviously big enough for their needs, since this creature managed to survive for over 10 million years.

Fast movers

NOT ALL DINOSAURS WERE HUGE and lumbering. Some were built for speed, either to run from attackers, or to chase prey. Unlike fast-running living animals like horses, which are all four-footed, fast-moving dinosaurs ran on their hind legs alone. As a result, all the fast movers looked similar. They all tended to have long back legs, in order to take long strides. Slender legs and narrow feet can be moved quickly and so allowed the dinosaurs to run more efficiently. The rest of the body was usually light and fairly short, balanced by a slender tail. The arms were lightly built, with small-clawed hands, and the neck was long, with a small head on top. Some of the nimble dinosaurs could reach speeds of 35 mph (56 kph) - almost as fast as a racehorse. They could take advantage of their speed in two ways: either to pursue a victim, or to beat a hasty retreat from an attacker. Herbivorous and carnivorous fast-moving dinosaurs were in a kind of "race": plant eaters became faster and faster because only the fastest could avoid being caught by ever-speedier meat eaters.

OSTRICH LOOKALIKE
Struthiomimus, or ostrich mimic, looked remarkably like an ostrich, and probably ran in a very similar way. The main difference is *Struthiomimus'* long bony tail and clawed hands (in place of an ostrich's feathered wings).

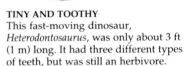

TINY AND TOOTHY
This fast-moving dinosaur, *Heterodontosaurus*, was only about 3 ft (1 m) long. It had three different types of teeth, but was still an herbivore.

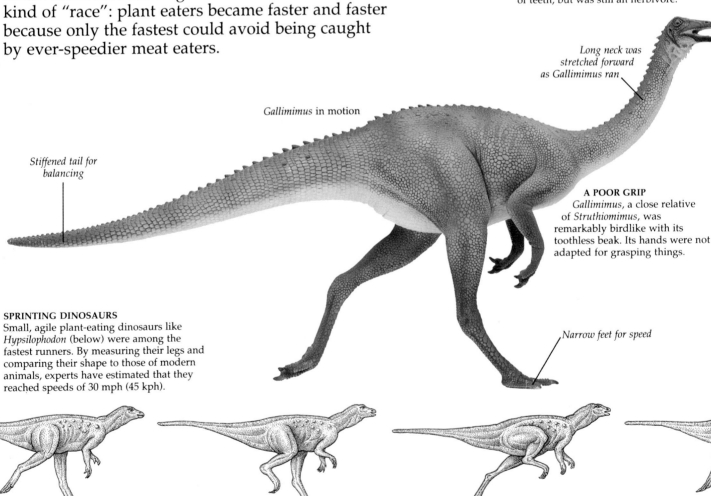

Long neck was stretched forward as Gallimimus ran

Gallimimus in motion

Stiffened tail for balancing

A POOR GRIP
Gallimimus, a close relative of *Struthiomimus*, was remarkably birdlike with its toothless beak. Its hands were not adapted for grasping things.

SPRINTING DINOSAURS
Small, agile plant-eating dinosaurs like *Hypsilophodon* (below) were among the fastest runners. By measuring their legs and comparing their shape to those of modern animals, experts have estimated that they reached speeds of 30 mph (45 kph).

Narrow feet for speed

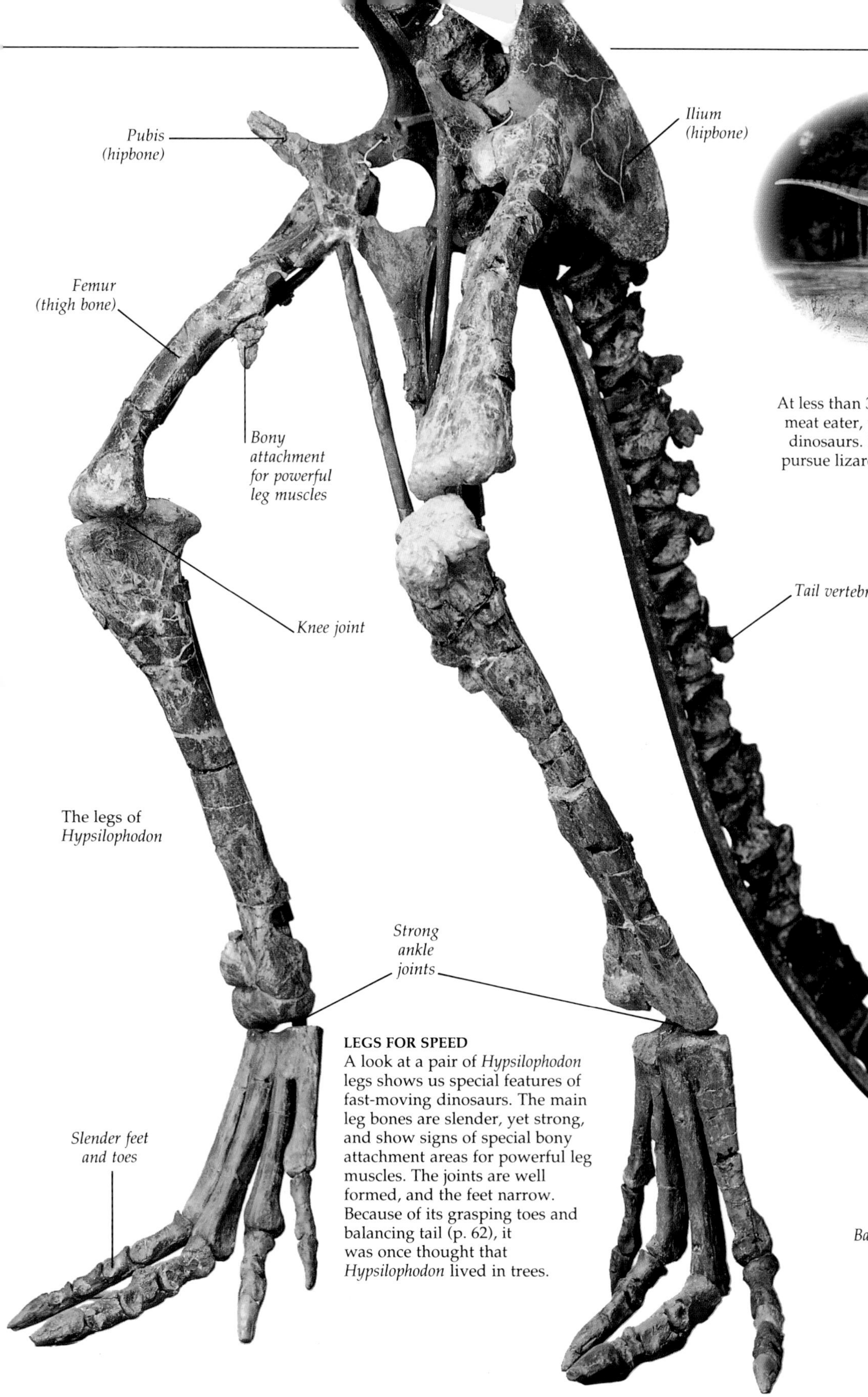

Pubis
(hipbone)

Ilium
(hipbone)

Femur
(thigh bone)

Bony
attachment
for powerful
leg muscles

Knee joint

Tail vertebra

The legs of
Hypsilophodon

Strong
ankle
joints

LEGS FOR SPEED
A look at a pair of *Hypsilophodon*
legs shows us special features of
fast-moving dinosaurs. The main
leg bones are slender, yet strong,
and show signs of special bony
attachment areas for powerful leg
muscles. The joints are well
formed, and the feet narrow.
Because of its grasping toes and
balancing tail (p. 62), it
was once thought that
Hypsilophodon lived in trees.

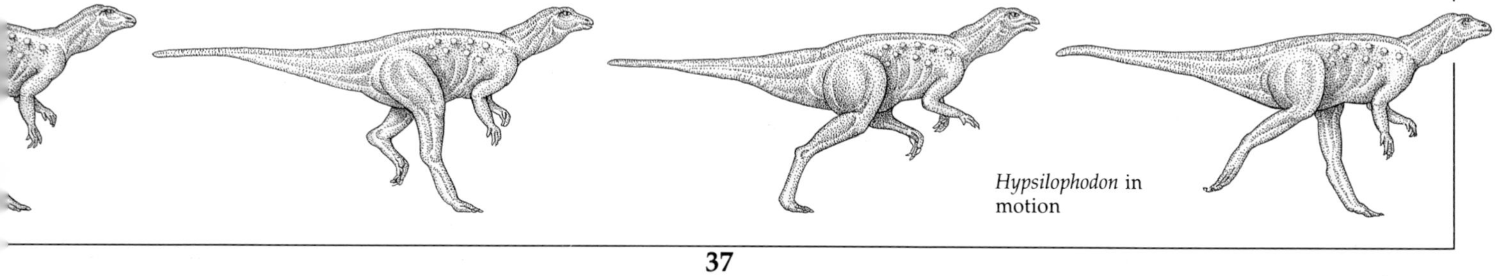

Slender feet
and toes

NIMBLE HUNTER
At less than 3 ft (1 m) long, *Compsognathus*, a
meat eater, was one of the smallest known
dinosaurs. It used its agility and speed to
pursue lizards, frogs, and a variety of other
small creatures.

**SPEEDY
BIRD**
Apart from
their long
tails, arms, and bare
skin, many of the
small, speedy dinosaurs
were just like ostriches.
Ostriches cannot fly,
but they can run as fast
as *Hypsilophodon* did.

Balancing
tail

Hypsilophodon in
motion

Two feet or four?

WHY DID SOME DINOSAURS WALK on four legs, and some on two? The answer is simply that dinosaurs walked in the way that suited their lifestyle best. Most carnivores, for instance, walked on their hind legs and used their hands to catch and hold on to their prey. Other dinosaurs walked on all four legs, mainly because their enormous size and weight needed support from four "posts" underneath - many of the large herbivores such as *Diplodocus* (p. 14) were like this. Some dinosaurs had the option of walking either on two or four legs, depending on what they were doing at the time. They could move around slowly on all fours, feeding on low vegetation, but when alarmed, could rear up and charge off on hind legs alone. These dinosaurs needed special "hands" that allowed for weight support, as well as grasping.

ON TWO LEGS ...
Corythosaurus, a hadrosaur (p. 28), most often adopted this pose, resting or walking on its hind legs. This left its small hands free to hold on to plants. *Corythosaurus* probably ran on its hind legs to escape predators like *Tyrannosaurus rex* (far right).

... AND ON FOUR
An examination of the hand bones of *Corythosaurus* reveals that several of the fingers ended in broad, flat hooves (right). These sorts of bones are typical of toes used for walking on, so *Corythosaurus* must have also walked on four legs sometimes.

TOE END
This hadrosaur toe bone from the "hand" is typically flat and hooflike.

Hadrosaur toe

Scelidosaurus foot

Hooflike claw

Anklebones

Triceratops toe

FOUR-LEGGED TOE
Triceratops always walked on four legs, so this *Triceratops* toe bone could come from either the front or the back foot. The toe bone is broader and more hooflike than that of the hadrosaur (above), which did not use its front feet so much.

SOMETHING AFOOT?
This is the complete hind foot of an early plant-eating dinosaur called *Scelidosaurus*. It was heavily armored with bony, jaw-breaking studs which ran the length of its body. *Scelidosaurus* always walked on four legs. Its hind foot was strong and broad and had four powerful toes to support the heavy body. The small first toe would have barely reached the ground.

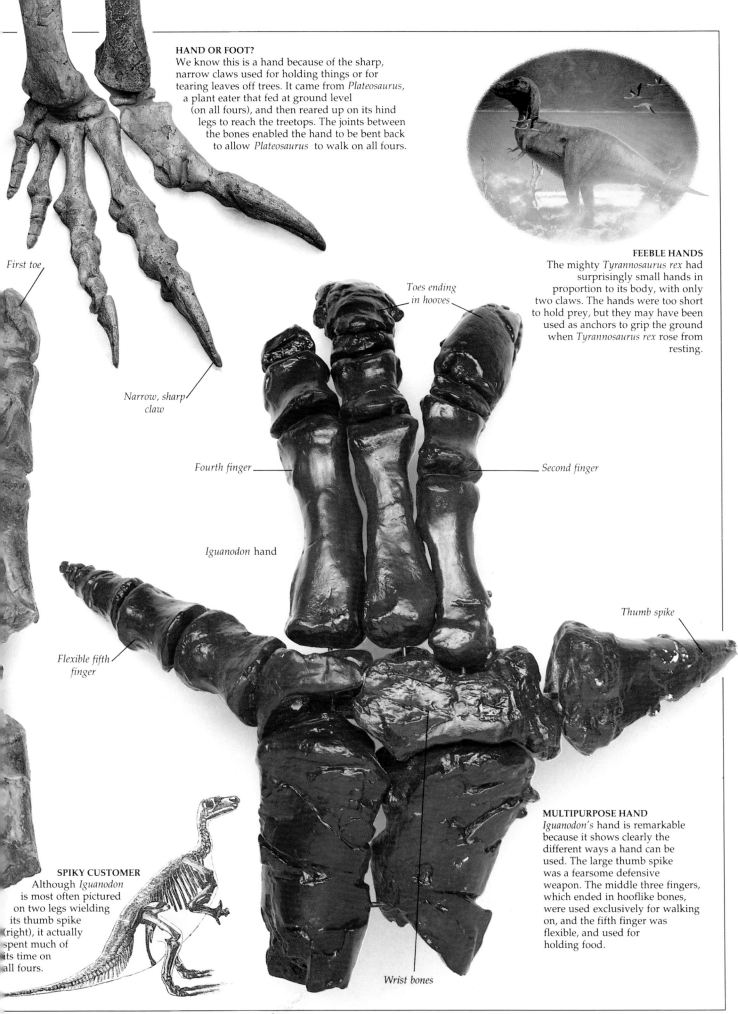

HAND OR FOOT?
We know this is a hand because of the sharp, narrow claws used for holding things or for tearing leaves off trees. It came from *Plateosaurus*, a plant eater that fed at ground level (on all fours), and then reared up on its hind legs to reach the treetops. The joints between the bones enabled the hand to be bent back to allow *Plateosaurus* to walk on all fours.

First toe

Narrow, sharp claw

FEEBLE HANDS
The mighty *Tyrannosaurus rex* had surprisingly small hands in proportion to its body, with only two claws. The hands were too short to hold prey, but they may have been used as anchors to grip the ground when *Tyrannosaurus rex* rose from resting.

Toes ending in hooves

Fourth finger

Second finger

Iguanodon hand

Thumb spike

Flexible fifth finger

SPIKY CUSTOMER
Although *Iguanodon* is most often pictured on two legs wielding its thumb spike (right), it actually spent much of its time on all fours.

MULTIPURPOSE HAND
Iguanodon's hand is remarkable because it shows clearly the different ways a hand can be used. The large thumb spike was a fearsome defensive weapon. The middle three fingers, which ended in hooflike bones, were used exclusively for walking on, and the fifth finger was flexible, and used for holding food.

Wrist bones

Ancient footprints

D INOSAURS NOT ONLY left fossilized bones as evidence of their existence, they also made their mark on the Earth with footprints. Tracks have been found where dinosaurs walked in soft, swampy land, like riverbanks, in search of food and water. Later on, the prints would have dried and hardened in the sun. Eventually, through rain or flooding, water would have brought more sand or mud which buried the prints until they gradually fossilized. They are called trace fossils because they are not actually a part of an animal. These footprints can tell us much about how dinosaurs traveled. For instance, a lot of the same types of prints found together with smaller ones in the middle suggests that some dinosaurs moved in herds, with the young ones protected in the center.

THE OWNE
OF THE PRIN
The huge footpri
on the right was mad
by an *Iguanodon* (p. 8
This plant eater ha
small hooves o
both its hand
and feet.
could wal
on two o
four fee

RUNNING ALL OVER THE WORLD
Dinosaur trackways have been found all over the world. These tracks found in Queensland, Australia, came from small meat eaters, running together as a pack. Experts can judge the speed at which they were moving by measuring the distance between the prints.

Toe bone

Iguanodon foot shown in reduced size

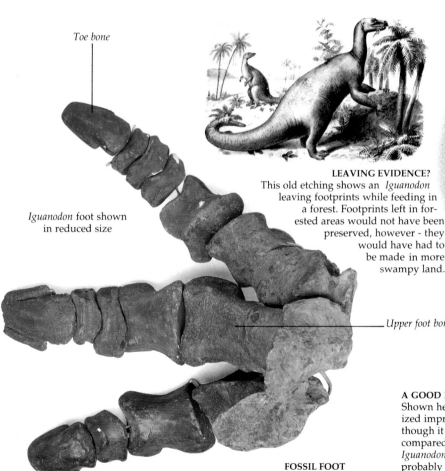

LEAVING EVIDENCE?
This old etching shows an *Iguanodon* leaving footprints while feeding in a forest. Footprints left in forested areas would not have been preserved, however - they would have had to be made in more swampy land.

Upper foot bone

A GOOD IMPRESSION
Shown here in almost life-size is part of the fossilized impression of an *Iguanodon's* left hind foot. Although it may seem huge, this footprint is quite small compared to some that have been found. A large, adult *Iguanodon* left footprints 36 in (90 cm) long. The creature probably weighed up to 2 tons. This print was probably made by a youngster weighing only about half a ton.

FOSSIL FOOT
The three-toed right foot of *Iguanodon* (above) had to be very strong to support the great weight of the animal. *Iguanodon* probably walked on its toes, like cats and dogs do today. The foot leaves a cloverleaf-shaped footprint, many of which have been found in southern England. The heavier the dinosaur, the better the footprint (right).

Iguanodon footprint

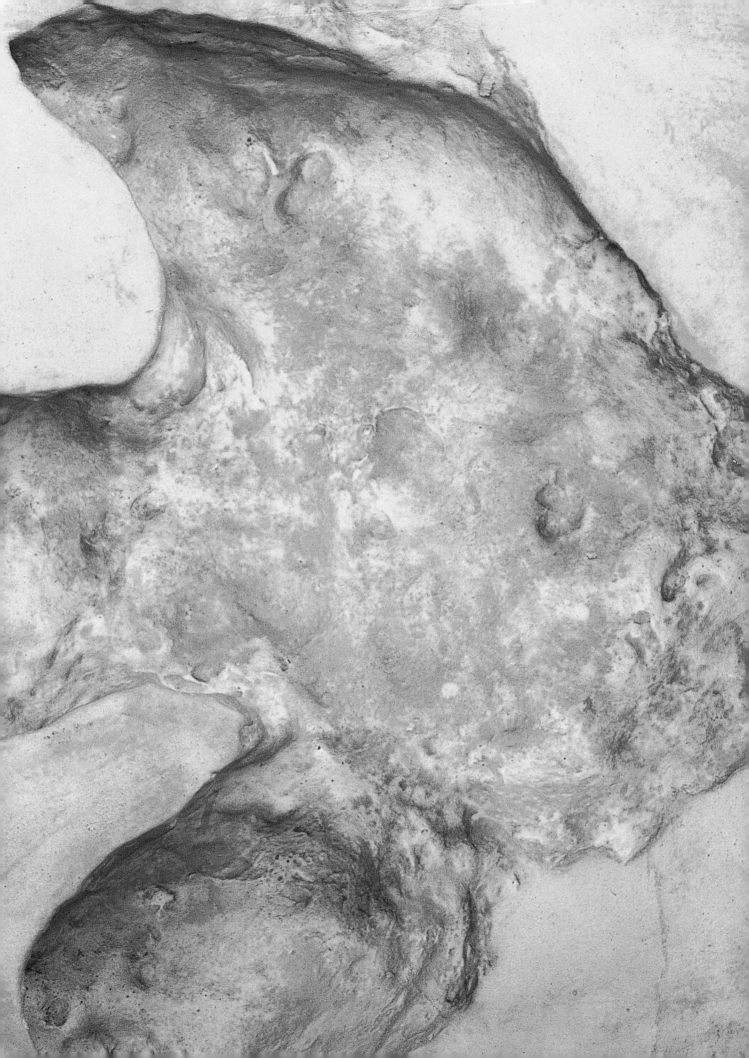

Claws and their uses

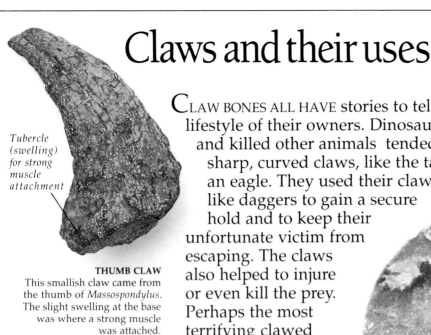

Tubercle
(swelling)
for strong
muscle
attachment

THUMB CLAW
This smallish claw came from the thumb of *Massospondylus*. The slight swelling at the base was where a strong muscle was attached.

CLAW BONES ALL HAVE stories to tell about the lifestyle of their owners. Dinosaurs that hunted and killed other animals tended to have very narrow, sharp, curved claws, like the talons on the foot of an eagle. They used their claws like daggers to gain a secure hold and to keep their unfortunate victim from escaping. The claws also helped to injure or even kill the prey. Perhaps the most terrifying clawed predator of the dinosaur age was *Deinonychus*, or "terrible claw." It had a huge sickle-like claw on its second toe, and long arms with three-clawed hands. It would leap on its victim and slash with its claws, using its long tail to keep its balance. Plant-eating and omnivorous dinosaurs, by contrast, did not have such sharp, talon-like claws. Their claws tended to be broader and more flattened, as they were not needed to kill. They were also stronger and more rugged because they were often put to many uses, such as walking, scraping, and digging for food. Sometimes these hooflike claws were used in self-defense, as crude weapons to slash out at attacking meat eaters.

"LEAPING LIZARDS"
Caught in action, with their teeth bared, these sparring meat eaters show how they best used their claws - for vicious attack!

ROAD RUNNER
From the picture it is easy to see why this dinosaur is called *Ornithomimus*, or ostrich dinosaur. Its main power lay in its long legs, which gave it the speed to beat a hasty retreat from pursuers, or to chase insects and small mammals. It probably used its claws and long fingers to search for food or to scratch in the earth for other dinosaurs' eggs.

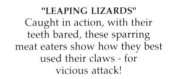

Flattened
claw

NOT FOR ATTACK
Although *Ornithomimus* was a meat eater, its claws were very flat, and would not have been much use for defense or attack.

FISHING TACKLE

This hand claw was found only recently in England, along with other remains of a meat-eating dinosaur named *Baryonyx*. The remarkable size and shape of the claw earned the newly discovered dinosaur the nickname "Claws." A flesh eater, it may have used its highly curved claw like a harpoon, to catch fish for its dinner!

Groove where horny covering was attached to claw

Baryonyx claw

ELEPHANT FEET

This huge claw came from a relative of *Diplodocus* (pp. 14-21) called *Apatosaurus*, a plant eater that walked on four pillar-like legs and had rounded feet, like an elephant's. Its claws were short and hooflike, except for the inside one on the front foot, shown here. This claw may have been used for digging, or even for defense.

Rough bone for attachment of heavy claw horn

FIGHTING TOOTH AND NAIL

Deinonychus was agile and intelligent. The males may have fought over females or territory, as shown here. Their stiff, bony tails were useful for balancing while leaping or pursuing a victim (p. 19).

Eggs and nests

A baby *Maiasaura* (p. 46) emerges from its egg

Dᴵɴᴏsᴀᴜʀs, ʟɪᴋᴇ ʀᴇᴘᴛɪʟᴇs ᴀɴᴅ ʙɪʀᴅs today, laid hard-shelled eggs. We know this because many fossilized dinosaur eggs have been found, some even containing small skeletons. Sometimes the eggs have been found in nests, with remains of the parent dinosaurs nearby. Nests found complete with fossilized young tell us that baby dinosaurs, like baby birds, would instinctively stay in their nest, no matter what happened to their mother. Several nests found close together suggest that some dinosaurs nested in colonies. It is perhaps surprising that dinosaur eggs were never very huge. If they were in proportion to the size of some adult dinosaurs, the shells would have been far too thick to hatch, and would not have allowed enough oxygen to reach the creatures growing inside.

Cracks which occurred during fossilization

Protoceratops egg

Unidentified dinosaur egg

Quail egg

BIRD AND DINOSAUR
When you consider that this quail's egg (left) would have hatched into a little bird, while the dinosaur egg (right) would have hatched into a massive creature, the size difference is not really so great!

Textured dinosaur eggshell

SPIKED LIZARD
Styracosaurus or "spiked lizard" was one of the bigger ceratopsians. *Protoceratops*, one of the earliest of the ceratopsian group, did not have any true horns, and would only have reached this dinosaur's knee (p. 46).

HARD SHELL
This elongated egg was laid by a *Protoceratops*, one of a group of dinosaurs called ceratopsians (pp. 30-31). Found in Mongolia in the 1920s, it was part of the first evidence that dinosaurs laid eggs. They laid their eggs on land, just like lizards do today. The amphibians, from which they evolved, had to lay their eggs in water, where they hatched into tadpoles. Reptiles, however, can lay their eggs on land because the eggs have tough shells with a private pond inside for the young to develop safely. Laying eggs like this was probably one of the reasons why the dinosaurs survived on Earth for so long.

BEAST'S NEST

e eggs in this sandy nest came from a
otoceratops. Several mothers laid their
gs in a circle in the same nest, which
ntained up to 30 eggs. They would
en have covered them with earth or
nd to protect them until they
tched. Fossils of baby, juvenile,
d adult *Protoceratops* have been
und close together, which suggests
ey may have lived in family groups.
me dinosaur nests, like those
ilt by the duckbills (p. 28),
d raised rims. These
others might have sat on
eir eggs, just like
ooding hens!

*est in which eggs
ere buried has turned
to sandstone through
ssilization process*

Birth and growth

BECAUSE MOST OF the dinosaurs were so big, it is hard to imagine them going through baby and juvenile stages in their lives. But recent discoveries have enabled us to piece together a little of their early lives. We know that dinosaur mothers laid their eggs in hollowed-out nests in the ground (pp. 44-45). In some cases, tiny skeletons of hatchlings have been found inside the eggs. Colonies of duckbill dinosaur nests have been found containing skeletons of hatchlings. Their teeth are worn, indicating that the mother dinosaur must have brought food back to the nest. Baby dinosaurs probably grew fast. Sauropods, which moved in herds (p. 12), probably kept their youngsters in the middle as they traveled, protected by the adults on the outside. Some dinosaurs, like the ceratopsians, changed their bodily proportions as they grew up.

THE NURSERY
Protoceratops (p. 45) made communal nests of 20 or more eggs, arranged in circles. This family scene shows baby *Protoceratops* at various stages - some hatching, some taking the first steps, and some struggling to get out of the sand!

Nostril

Flat nose ridge

Orbit (eye socket)

Nostril

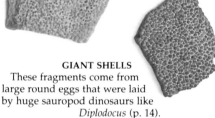

Sauropod eggshell fragments

GIANT SHELLS
These fragments come from large round eggs that were laid by huge sauropod dinosaurs like *Diplodocus* (p. 14).

A BEAST EMERGES
This fossilized eggshell (left) contains a hatchling duckbill dinosaur called *Maiasaura*, or "good mother lizard." It was found recently in Montana along with hundreds of other dinosaur eggs and babies. It is shown here at life-size - small enough to fit in an adult's hand.

Protoceratops eggshell fragments

COARSE SHELLS
The coarse, bumpy surface of these *Protoceratops* shell fragments is typical of many dinosaur eggs.

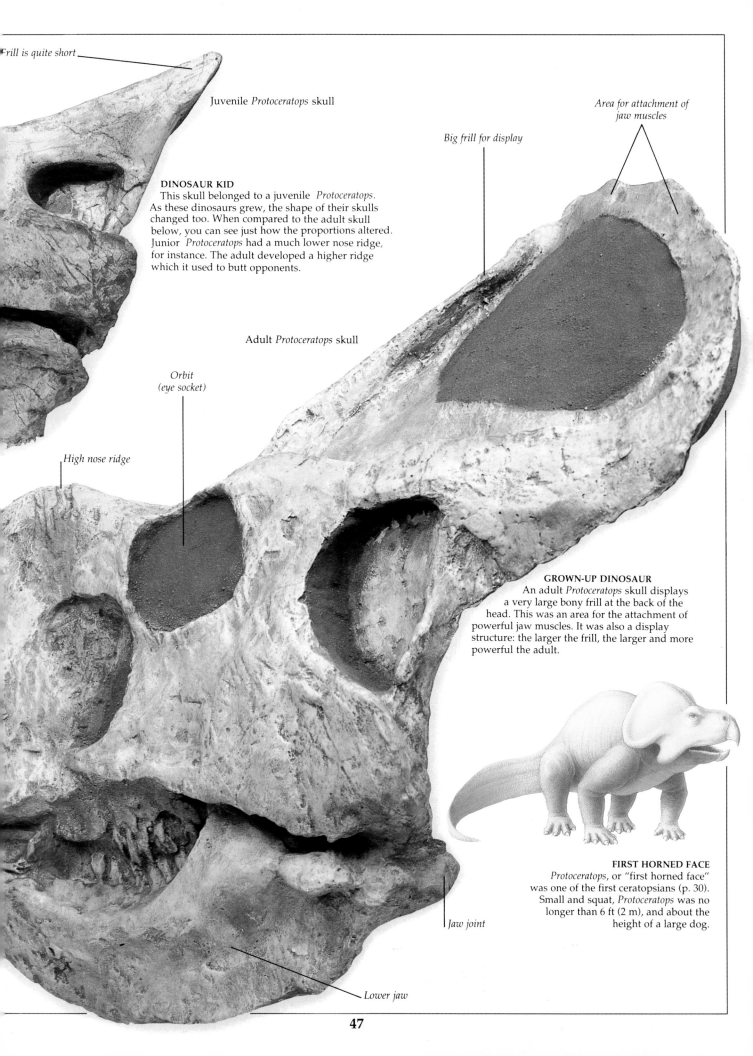

Frill is quite short

Juvenile *Protoceratops* skull

Area for attachment of
jaw muscles

Big frill for display

DINOSAUR KID
This skull belonged to a juvenile *Protoceratops*.
As these dinosaurs grew, the shape of their skulls
changed too. When compared to the adult skull
below, you can see just how the proportions altered.
Junior *Protoceratops* had a much lower nose ridge,
for instance. The adult developed a higher ridge
which it used to butt opponents.

Adult *Protoceratops* skull

Orbit
(eye socket)

High nose ridge

GROWN-UP DINOSAUR
An adult *Protoceratops* skull displays
a very large bony frill at the back of the
head. This was an area for the attachment of
powerful jaw muscles. It was also a display
structure: the larger the frill, the larger and more
powerful the adult.

FIRST HORNED FACE
Protoceratops, or "first horned face"
was one of the first ceratopsians (p. 30).
Small and squat, *Protoceratops* was no
longer than 6 ft (2 m), and about the
height of a large dog.

Jaw joint

Lower jaw

47

Death of the dinosaurs

DINOSAURS DISAPPEARED from the Earth quite suddenly, and why this happened is still a mystery. Around 70 million years ago, the dinosaurs ruled the Earth. Yet about five million years later, they had all died out, perhaps only in a matter of months. Scientists have offered various theories to explain their sudden extinction, but many ignore one vital point: dinosaurs were only one of a whole range of creatures that died out at the same time, including all the swimming and flying reptiles. So any theory to explain dinosaur extinction must explain the disappearance of these groups as well. The theories are numerous: some people think that small mammals ate all the dinosaur eggs. This is very unlikely - for how would it account for the extinction of other species that disappeared at the same time? Others believe that a plague of caterpillars ate all the dinosaurs' plant food, and they starved to death.

POISONOUS BITE
It has been suggested that dinosaurs died out because they ate new kinds of poisonous plants, such as deadly nightshade, that started growing on Earth.

Stony meteorite fragment

ROCKS FROM SPACE
A likely reason for the sudden extinction is that a massive meteorite from space collided with the Earth. This would have been catastrophic, causing a huge steam and dust cloud which darkened the Earth for a long time, killing off the plants and the animals that fed on them.

Fossilized ammonite

Iron meteorite fragment

A MASS EXTINCTION
Many other creatures died out at the time of the dinosaur extinction. Whatever happened seemed to affect some creatures and leave others unharmed. Ammonites, a type of shellfish, became extinct, as did the mosasaurs, plesiosaurs, and ichthyosaurs, groups of meat-eating marine reptiles. Sea crocodiles died out but the river crocodiles survived. Pterosaurs, (flying reptiles), disappeared, but birds were unaffected.

Iguanodon ischium (hipbone)

Shaft of ischium bent forward after repair

Section of
hadrosaur backbone

*Vertebral
spine*

**THE BEGINNING
OF THE END**
A *Tyrannosaurus rex*
is shown fleeing in
terror as a meteor hits
the Earth. The impact
would have had an effect
kind of like that of a massive
nuclear war. Dense black clouds of dust and
soot would have cut out the sun for months.

A GROWTH
Dinosaurs could contract cancer. This section of backbone
belonged to a hadrosaur, and shows a swollen area
which was a cancerous tumor in the bone.

*Point of
fracture*

*Thickening of
bone around break*

*Vertebral
body*

*Swollen area of
tumor growth*

BROKEN BONE
During their reign, dinosaurs were not immune to diseases
and accidents. The *Iguanodon* hipbone above shows a fracture
that healed itself during the creature's lifetime.

Dinosaur or bird?

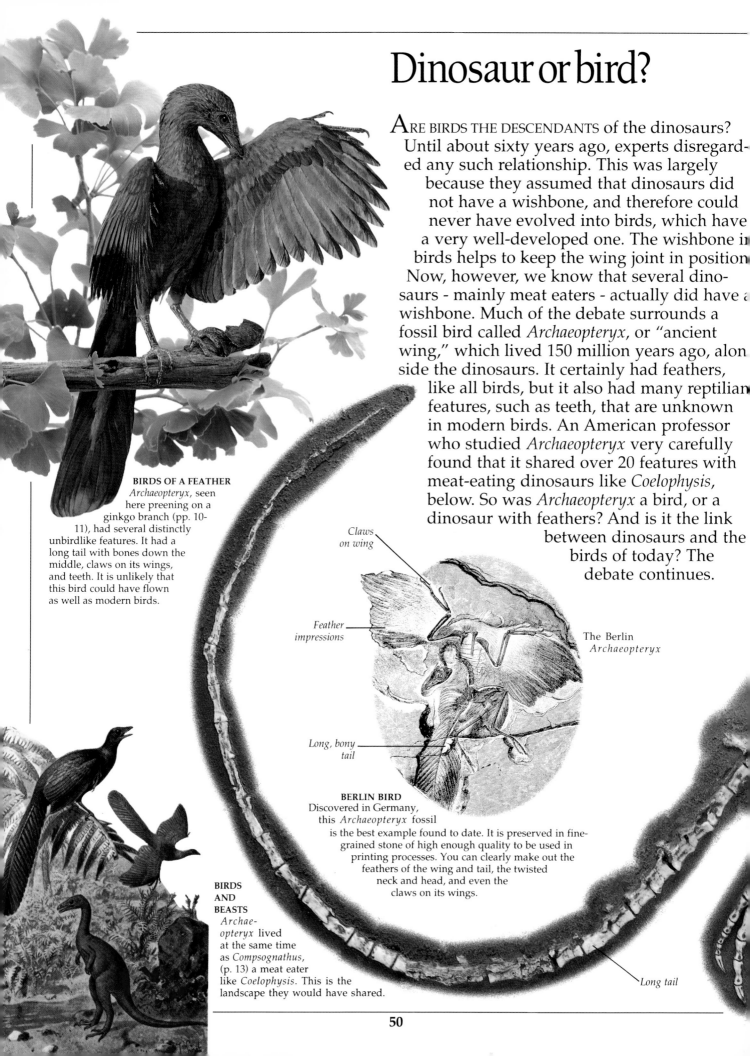

ARE BIRDS THE DESCENDANTS of the dinosaurs? Until about sixty years ago, experts disregarded any such relationship. This was largely because they assumed that dinosaurs did not have a wishbone, and therefore could never have evolved into birds, which have a very well-developed one. The wishbone in birds helps to keep the wing joint in position. Now, however, we know that several dinosaurs - mainly meat eaters - actually did have a wishbone. Much of the debate surrounds a fossil bird called *Archaeopteryx*, or "ancient wing," which lived 150 million years ago, along-side the dinosaurs. It certainly had feathers, like all birds, but it also had many reptilian features, such as teeth, that are unknown in modern birds. An American professor who studied *Archaeopteryx* very carefully found that it shared over 20 features with meat-eating dinosaurs like *Coelophysis*, below. So was *Archaeopteryx* a bird, or a dinosaur with feathers? And is it the link between dinosaurs and the birds of today? The debate continues.

BIRDS OF A FEATHER
Archaeopteryx, seen here preening on a ginkgo branch (pp. 10-11), had several distinctly unbirdlike features. It had a long tail with bones down the middle, claws on its wings, and teeth. It is unlikely that this bird could have flown as well as modern birds.

Claws on wing

Feather impressions

Long, bony tail

The Berlin *Archaeopteryx*

BERLIN BIRD
Discovered in Germany, this *Archaeopteryx* fossil is the best example found to date. It is preserved in fine-grained stone of high enough quality to be used in printing processes. You can clearly make out the feathers of the wing and tail, the twisted neck and head, and even the claws on its wings.

BIRDS AND BEASTS
Archae-opteryx lived at the same time as *Compsognathus*, (p. 13) a meat eater like *Coelophysis*. This is the landscape they would have shared.

Long tail

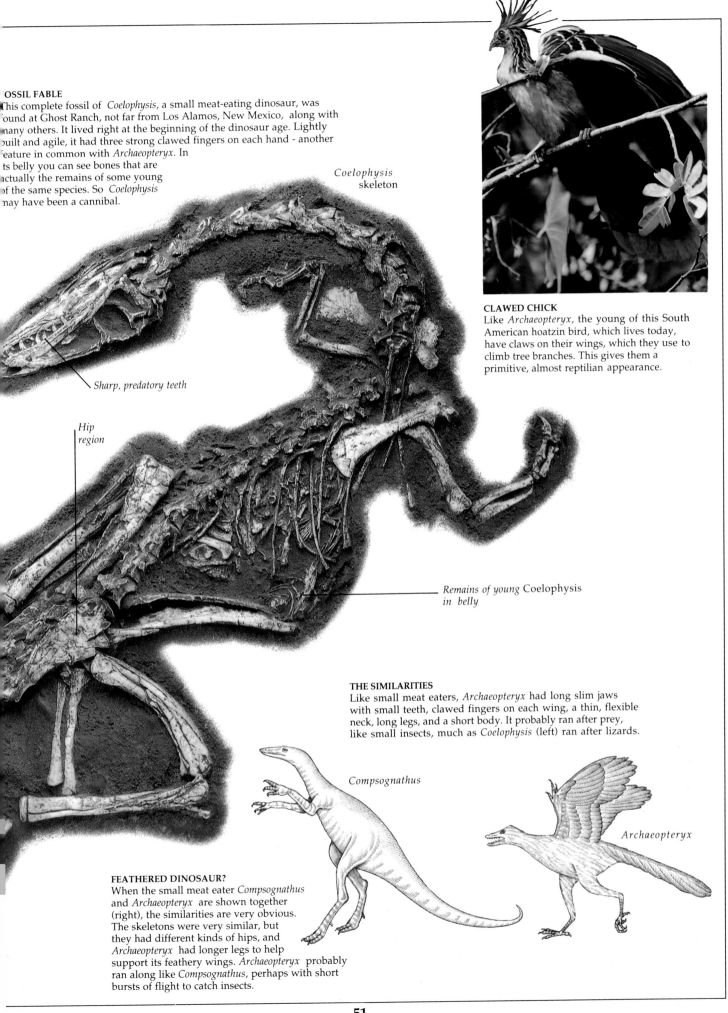

FOSSIL FABLE

This complete fossil of *Coelophysis*, a small meat-eating dinosaur, was
found at Ghost Ranch, not far from Los Alamos, New Mexico, along with
many others. It lived right at the beginning of the dinosaur age. Lightly
built and agile, it had three strong clawed fingers on each hand - another
feature in common with *Archaeopteryx*. In
its belly you can see bones that are
actually the remains of some young
of the same species. So *Coelophysis*
may have been a cannibal.

Coelophysis
skeleton

Sharp, predatory teeth

*Hip
region*

CLAWED CHICK

Like *Archaeopteryx*, the young of this South
American hoatzin bird, which lives today,
have claws on their wings, which they use to
climb tree branches. This gives them a
primitive, almost reptilian appearance.

Remains of young Coelophysis
in belly

THE SIMILARITIES

Like small meat eaters, *Archaeopteryx* had long slim jaws
with small teeth, clawed fingers on each wing, a thin, flexible
neck, long legs, and a short body. It probably ran after prey,
like small insects, much as *Coelophysis* (left) ran after lizards.

Compsognathus

Archaeopteryx

FEATHERED DINOSAUR?

When the small meat eater *Compsognathus*
and *Archaeopteryx* are shown together
(right), the similarities are very obvious.
The skeletons were very similar, but
they had different kinds of hips, and
Archaeopteryx had longer legs to help
support its feathery wings. *Archaeopteryx* probably
ran along like *Compsognathus*, perhaps with short
bursts of flight to catch insects.

How to find a dinosaur

HOW DO SCIENTISTS go about discovering dinosaur remains? Because the dinosaurs became fossilized in the first place by being buried in sand, or mud, we know that their fossils can only be found in sedimentary rock - rock that has been built up in layers over the years. Sometimes fossils are found by accident for example by builders digging into the ground. Or fossil collectors may set out deliberately to search an area that is thought to be rich in fossils. Sometimes a large and highly organized scientific expedition is undertaken, based on detailed research. Whatever the method of discovery, careful preparation must be done if the find is to be recovered successfully. Records need to be made of the exact position of the find. And the right tools are needed to ensure that the fossils are removed from the site and returned to the laboratory without being damaged.

THE FIND!
Discoveries of fossil dinosaurs are rare, and best tackled by a team of experienced people.

DUTCH DISCOVERY
The jaws of the mighty sea lizard *Mosasaurus* were discovered deep in a chalk mine near Maastricht in Holland in 1770. This etching shows the team of discoverers working by torchlight.

Gloves

PROTECTIVE GEAR
It is essential to wear proper protective clothing while on a fossil dig. Gloves are needed when heavy hammering and chiseling are done, and goggles are used to protect the eyes from splinters of rock. A hard hat is also advisable, especially if work is being done near cliffs.

TAKING NOTE
On a dig, paleontologists always record details of a find and draw a map of the site. Broken fragments and samples of rock are collected in bags and analyzed later back in the laboratory.

HAMMERS
A variety of hammers are used by paleontologists (fossil experts) in the field. The geological hammers shown here are good at splitting fossil-bearing rock.

Straight-headed hammer for splitting hard rock

Cloth bags

Curved-headed brick hammer for breaking up and clearing softer rock such as clay.

Rock saw for cutting through rock

Hard hat and
protective goggles

RIBS IN A JACKET
When fossils are partly
exposed, they are sometimes
encased in plaster jackets to
protect them for transportation
back to the laboratory. Two
ribs of the recently discovered
dinosaur *Baryonyx* can be seen
in this jacket (pp. 54-55).

Pot of glue

POT AND BRUSHES
Brushes are used to clear
away dust while rock is
being chipped away
around fossils. As a fossil
is exposed, it is often
painted with a hardener,
such as glue, to secure any
loose fragments.

Soft
paintbrush

Baryonyx ribs
encased in plaster jacket

*Aluminum foil
covers fossil*

Lump hammer

PROTECTING THE FIND
A paleontologist on a dig
carefully covers a fossil with
a plaster jacket.

Pointed chisels

Flat chisels

Plastic
bags

EXPOSING A FIND
When the rock in
which the fossil is
embedded is very
hard, a heavy hammer
and chisels are needed.
This lump hammer is
used to drive chisels into
the rock. It is useful to
have a wide variety of
chisels for getting into
awkward corners.

FOAM JACKET
Sometimes fossils are protected by
a polyurethane foam jacket. The
fossil is first wrapped in foil, then
the chemicals to make the foam are poured
over it. The foam expands and surrounds the
fossil, which can then be moved safely.
Because foam gives off toxic gases as it
is mixed, it is not recommended for use
except by professionals.

Clipboard with
drawing of the
site, and notebook
with field notes

Hard paintbrush

Polyurethane
foam jacket

RAW MATERIALS
To make a plaster jacket, the plaster
is mixed with water to make a paste,
then the scrim is dipped into it. The
rock and fossil are covered with a
layer of wet tissue paper before the
scrim and plaster are applied. This
keeps the plaster from sticking
to the rock and fossil.

Roll of plasterer's scrim
(open-weave fabric),
and plaster of Paris

How to rebuild a dinosaur

AFTER THE hard work of excavation, the precious fossils are taken back to the laboratory for preparation, study, and display. This whole process is a lengthy one. First the fossil remains need to be carefully removed from their protective jackets (p. 53). Then the remaining rock or earth in which the fossil was originally buried has to be cleaned away. Chisels are used on hard pieces of rock, and more delicate power-driven tools (like dentists' drills) are used for detailed work. Sometimes chemicals are used to dissolve away the excess rock. The cleaned bones are then carefully studied to figure out how they fitted together, and therefore understand how the dinosaur lived. Some clues are found on the actual surface of bones, because muscles sometimes leave clear marks where they were attached. These marks can be used to reconstruct dinosaur muscles.

READY TO DISPLAY
The laboratory workers shown here are putting the finishing touches to what has probably been months or even years of work cleaning and preparing this fossil skeleton.

Iguanodon foot bone

Cartilage cap of ankle joint

Ligament scars

CLUES FROM THE BONE
This foot bone from *Iguanodon* provides many clues of muscle attachment during life. At the upper left end its surface is roughened for attachment of cartilage (gristle) of the ankle joint, and along its length are ligament scars for attachment to other bones. The rough area at the bottom of the bone is a cartilage joint surface for the middle toe

Cartilage surface of joint for toe

Adding the flesh

Once all the bones of the dinosaur's skeleton have been cleaned, scientists can attempt a reconstruction of the body. It may take some time to work out how the bones fitted together, and missing bones may have to be modeled from plaster. Then the "flesh" can be added, based on detailed knowledge of how the dinosaur's muscles were arranged. This is established by studying "muscle scars" on the bones and comparing them with the bones of living reptiles.

FINISHING TOUCH
Many hours of work in the field and laboratory by scientists and the model-maker have gone into the fleshed-out dinosaur model shown here.

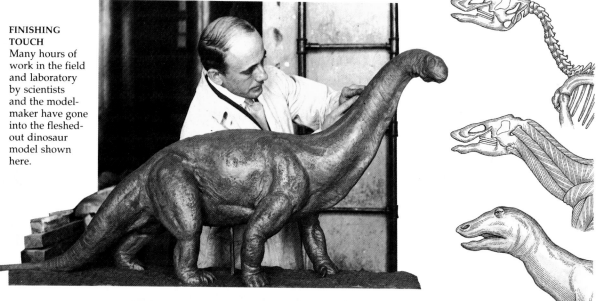

RECONSTRUCTED SKELETON
Once the skeleton has been put together, an attempt at fleshing out the dinosaur can begin. A special scientific artist makes sketches to help the model-maker.

MUSCLING IN
By studying the bones, the muscles can be added as accurately as possible.

ADDING THE SKIN
Finally, the skin is added. This is more difficult, but skin impressions are sometimes preserved (p. 32). Color is a matter of guesswork.

Baryonyx neck
vertebra

*Faint
scratches*

A LOAD OF OLD BONES
During the 19th century, when dinosaurs had just been
discovered (pp. 8-9), the sculptor Benjamin Waterhouse
Hawkins built models of dinosaurs first in England,
then in the United States. This shows his work-
shop in New York.

NECK BONE
his neck bone
elonged to the
ewly discovered dinosaur
aryonyx, seen reconstructed
pposite. The bone has a
omplicated shape and
vas buried in very hard rock,
o it took a long time to
repare. The faint scratches
hat can be seen are where
ock remains to be cleared.

AN ACID BATH
Sometimes, in laboratories,
vats of acid are used to dissolve away rock from fossils
without damaging them. The
chemicals used in this process
can be very dangerous, so protective clothing must always be worn
when lowering the fossil into the vat.

N DEATH THROES
Baryonyx is shown here as it looked
fter it died. It sank to the bottom
of a lake where it gradually
ecame fossilized. Such a
realistic model shows how
he skills of the scientist
nd model-maker can be
prought together to great
effect. The way that
the dinosaur was lying
was worked out from
the position in which
the bones were found.

Model of *Baryonyx* as it looked after it died

The timescale

IT IS INCREDIBLE TO THINK that animals and plants have lived on Earth for over 700 million years. During this time a bewildering variety has come and gone. The first dinosaurs appeared about 210 million years ago (mya) at the end of what is known as the Triassic period. They roamed the Earth throughout the Jurassic period until 64 million years ago, right at the end of the Cretaceous period. During the millions of years of life on Earth, the world has changed enormously: continents have moved, sea levels and climates have changed, creatures have become extinct. If we look at fossils of creatures that lived before, during, and after the dinosaur age, we can see how some things have changed, and some have remained much the same.

At the time when the dinosaurs appeared, none of the countries of the world existed as we know them - the world consisted of one huge landmass called Pangaea.

TRILOBITE
This creature lived on the seabed and scuttled around on sharp, spiny legs. Although abundant in the early oceans, it was extinct long before the first dinosaurs appeared.

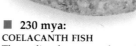

IN THE MISTS OF TIME
This is what the world may have looked like during the dinosaur age. Dinosaurs lived through three periods of time: the Triassic, from 230 to 195 mya, the Jurassic, from 195 to 141 mya, and the Cretaceous, from 141 to 65 mya.

A BEETLE
Beetles are a group with a very long history, and were probably the prey of early reptiles and amphibians, just as they are today.

Small sharp teeth

■ **260 mya:**
AMPHIBIAN
Amphibians lived before and during the dinosaur age, and are still with us today. Frogs, for instance, are amphibians. They can breathe and move on land, but have to lay their eggs in water (p. 44).

■ **260 mya:**
EARLY REPTILE
This is the underside of the skull of an early lizard-like reptile called *Captorhinus*. It may have eaten small insects and snails with its small sharp teeth.

■ **230 mya:**
COELACANTH FISH
The earliest known coelacanth appeared 390 million years ago. These fish were thought to be extinct, but recently many living coelacanths have been discovered.

Spaces for jaw muscles

SCORPION STORY
Living scorpions belong to an ancient group which dates back about 400 million years.

■ **230 mya:**
DIICTODON
The owner of this mammal-like reptile skull was squat and pig-shaped. It ate plants and lived during the early Triassic period.

■ **230 mya:**
PROCOLOPHON
This is the skull of a small early reptile which fed on roots and tubers.

LIVING FOSSIL
This lungfish has fossil relatives which date back 390 million years.

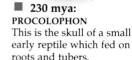

■ **200 mya:**
MEGAZOSTRODON:
This furry model is based on a tiny skeleton that was found a few years ago. It was one of the earliest true mammals, and lived alongside the early dinosaurs.

Eye socket

■ **205 mya:**
MASSETOGNATHUS
The last mammal-like reptiles that appeared just before the early dinosaurs were large and doglike in appearance. Mammal-like reptiles became extinct when the dinosaurs appeared, but smaller, rodent-like mammals survived.

■ **200 mya:**
ICHTHYOSAUR
Ichthyosaurs were swimming reptiles which flourished throughout the dinosaur age. This paddle - once a limb - would have been used by the animal to propel itself along in the water. Ichthyosaurs had long, narrow, pointed snouts.

Long narrow snout

■ **200 mya:**
CROCODILE
The shape of a crocodile skull has not changed very much over the years. A long snout lined with teeth is one of the best tools for catching swimming prey. The snout on this crocodile is particularly narrow, which suggests that it must have been very partial to fish.

■ **210 mya:**
RIOJASUCHUS
This skull belonged to a creature that lived just before the early dinosaurs, one of the thecodonts or "socket toothed" reptiles. It was built like a long-legged crocodile, and had powerful teeth and jaws.

The story continues. . .

Two Thecodontosaurus feeding

■ **200 mya:**
THECODONTOSAURUS
This fragment of jaw belonged to an early dinosaur. Most early dinosaur fossils are poorly preserved.

STAYING POWER
Crocodiles lived before, during, and after the reign of the dinosaurs, and are still around today. Being aggressive river-dwelling predators obviously suits them very well.

EARLY DAYS
Thecodontosaurus could eat both plants and meat (p. 23). One of these two is feeding on cycads; the other is about to pounce on a lizard.

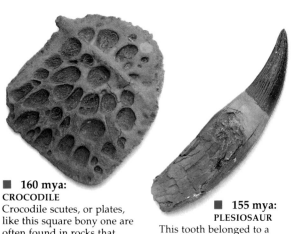

■ **160 mya:**
CROCODILE
Crocodile scutes, or plates, like this square bony one are often found in rocks that also yield dinosaur remains. This suggests that crocodiles may have scavenged dinosaur carcasses.

■ **155 mya:**
PLESIOSAUR
This tooth belonged to a plesiosaur, a fierce marine reptile that lived at the same time as ichthyosaurs (p. 57). They lived during the Jurassic period.

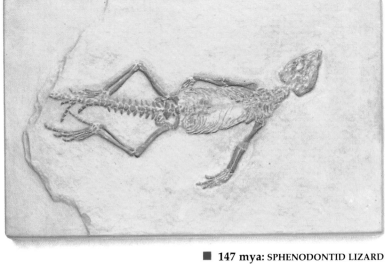

■ **147 mya:** SPHENODONTID LIZARD
Lizard-like reptiles such as this specimen have a very long history. They lived throughout the reign of the dinosaurs.

Modern dragonfly

Fossil dragonfly

■ **140 mya:**
DATED DRAGONFLY
Dragonflies can be called "living fossils": they were flying in the skies 320 million years ago, and still exist today.

■ **140 mya:**
KING CRAB
King crabs are only remotely related to crabs. They have been around since before the dinosaur age, and still live today.

Gray plover

DAWN OF THE BIRDS
The first birds appeared in the late Jurassic period - about 150 mya. But they did not come into their own and rule the skies until the pterosaurs became extinct (at the same time as the dinosaurs).

■ **140 mya:**
GRYODUS
Many types of bony fish like this one lived at the same time as the dinosaurs. Most were fossilized in fine lake sediments, so they are preserved in great detail.

■ **145 mya:**
PTERODACTYLUS
Flying reptiles called pterosaurs flew in the skies while the dinosaurs ruled the land. Some were the size of sparrows; others were as big as small aircraft. The larger ones would have swooped down to catch fish in the waters, while smaller ones, like this *Pterodactylus* (right), would have caught insects in the air.

The cockroach is one of nature's great survivors. Cockroaches have lived on Earth since long before the dinosaur age, and, judging by their success at living in human environments, they seem set to survive for a long time to come.

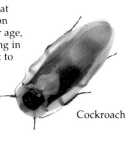

Cockroach

COME FLY...
In the Jurassic Period, a sky scene at dawn or dusk would have been crowded with pterosaurs darting through the air catching prey. Their place is taken today by birds that feed on the wing: swifts, housemartins, and swallows.

■ 136 mya:
DRYOSAURUS
This femur (thigh bone) belonged to a small, fast-moving, plant-eating dinosaur. It used its speed to flee fierce predators.

Dryosaurus femur

Water moccasin snake

SNAKES ON THE SCENE
Slithering snakes arrived on the scene in the late Cretaceous period. They are like modified legless lizards.

■ 120 mya:
LIZARD'S JAW
This fragment of jaw came from a lizard like the sphenodontid preserved in rock, above left. Fragments like this are found more often than complete specimens.

■ 120 mya:
CROCODILE
The crocodile that owned this skull (right) lived in the early Cretaceous period.

■ 115 mya:
IGUANODON
This is a tail bone from *Iguanodon*, a plant-eating dinosaur (pp. 8-9). *Iguanodon* lived only in the Cretaceous period.

■ 120 mya: TEETH
These fierce-looking stumpy crocodile teeth are preserved from 120 million years ago, but are very like the teeth that belong to living crocodiles today.

The story continues. . .

■ 120 mya:
SCUTE
This scute, part of a crocodile's bony armor, comes from a crocodile that lived during the Cretaceous period.

■ 110 mya:
GASTROPOD
Many different snails lived during the dinosaur age.

The end of an era

As THE CRETACEOUS PERIOD drew to a close, the dinosaurs became gradually less numerous, until eventually they disappeared altogether. At the same time changes were also taking place in the Earth's landscape. The continents became separated by wide stretches of sea. Sea levels rose, flooding much of the low-lying land where many types of dinosaur lived. Many groups of sea animals became extinct. Instead of being warm all the time, the climate began to become more variable, or seasonal. The types of plants living at the time also changed: flowering plants became increasingly abundant. As the dinosaurs died out, they made way for a new ruling group on Earth: the mammals.

70 mya:
MOSASAUR
This giant marine lizard used its large pointed teeth to crack open shells of animals such as ammonites (p. 48).

NOT LONG TO LIVE
The mosasaurs lived only at the end of the Cretaceous period, and became extinct alongside the dinosaurs.

Turtle shell

95 mya:
TURTLE
This turtle shell is a relic from the Cretaceous period. Turtles were another group that survived the mass extinction.

90 mya:
ALBERTOSAURUS
The owner of this toe bone was a large meat-eating dinosaur. Few of these meat eaters survived up to the end of the dinosaur age.

100 mya:
ICHTHYOSAUR
These sharp, pointed teeth, now embedded in rock, belonged to an ichthyosaur (p. 57). Marine reptiles like this all became extinct at the same time as the dinosaurs.

Scales

75 mya:
CRAB
Crabs, like their lobster relatives, survived the extinction (p. 58).

Crab

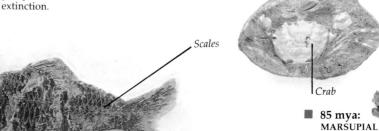

85 mya:
MARSUPIAL
This jaw bone belonged to a pouched mammal (like a kangaroo). Marsupials, now found mainly in Australia, lived alongside the dinosaurs, and were able to evolve rapidly after they disappeared.

90 mya:
BONY FISH
Bony ray-finned fish were another group that suffered very little damage during the "great extinction."

100 mya:
LOBSTER
Some marine groups, like lobsters, were barely affected by the mass extinction at the end of the Cretaceous period. Why some groups became extinct and others didn't is to this day a great mystery.

100 mya:
LEAF
Broad leaves like this one are typical of flowering plants that appeared during the Cretaceous period.

BONY HERRING
The bony fish we are familiar with today are very like those that lived in the late Cretaceous.

Hawksbill turtle

1 mya:
HOMO ERECTUS
Human beings were one of the last species to arrive on the ever-changing scene on Earth. Early species of humans date back a mere one million years (64 million years after the last dinosaur died). In this "short" period of time, people have risen to dominate most of the land and are beginning to have a notice-able effect on the environment.

Human skull

URTLE TALE
urtles and
ortoises belong to
group of reptiles
at have changed
ery little in appearance
nce their origins 200
illion years ago.

55 mya:
TURTLE SKULL

25 mya:
SHARK TOOTH
Sharks have been around for 400 million years and have changed very little.

A BRACHIOPOD
Brachiopods, or lampshells, one of the oldest animal groups, are little changed from those found in rocks 500 million years old.

Cricket

Spider

Hyracotherium
(early horse) skull

35 mya:
INSECTS IN AMBER
This cricket and spider were perfectly preserved millions of years ago, because they became trapped in amber, fossilized resin that drips from pine trees.

Early rodent skull

35 mya:
EARLY RODENT
Gnawing animals like rats and mice did not exist until well after the dinosaurs died, and are still thriving today.

40 mya:
LIZARD
This jaw belonged to a land lizard. Although all the giant marine lizards like mosasaurs (pp. 48 and 60) became extinct with the dinosaurs, the small land-living ones were unaffected.

50 mya:
EARLY HORSE
Horses appeared soon after the dinosaurs became extinct, and soon there were many different types of horses grazing on the new plants and grasses that were growing. Early horses had toes, not hooves, on their feet.

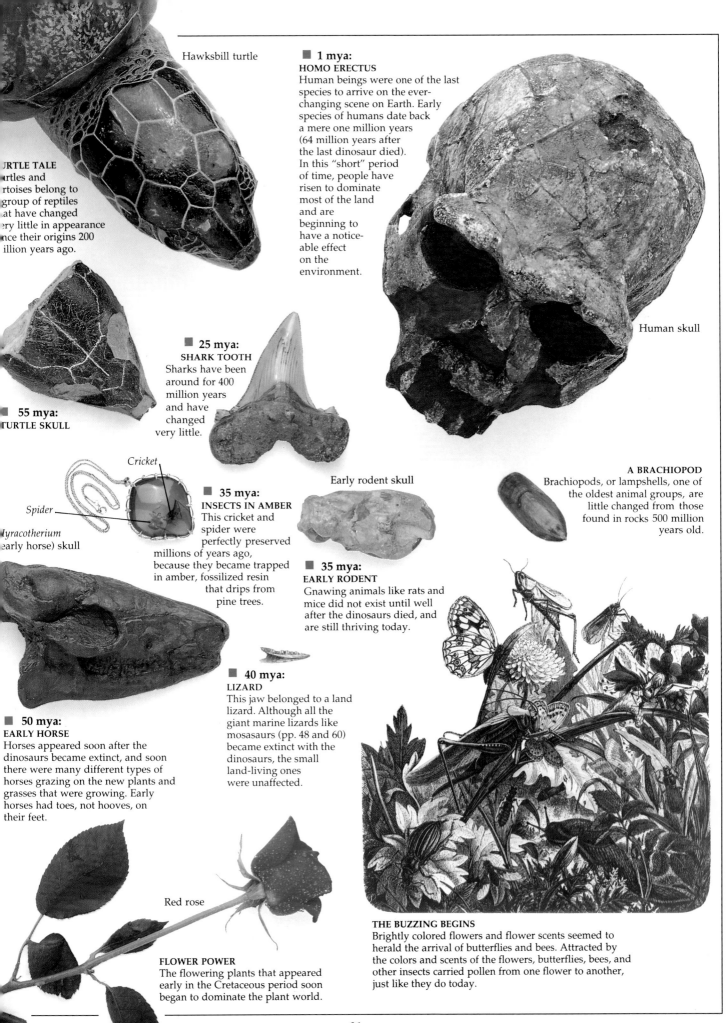

Red rose

FLOWER POWER
The flowering plants that appeared early in the Cretaceous period soon began to dominate the plant world.

THE BUZZING BEGINS
Brightly colored flowers and flower scents seemed to herald the arrival of butterflies and bees. Attracted by the colors and scents of the flowers, butterflies, bees, and other insects carried pollen from one flower to another, just like they do today.

Myths and legends

W HEN DINOSAUR BONES were first discovered, people found it hard to believe that these creatures had actually lived on Earth. They associated the dinosaurs with terrifying monsters. Because so little was known about them, many mistakes were made at the beginning. Dinosaur bones were put together in the wrong way (p. 8), or even mixed up with other creatures' bones. Today, misconceptions about dinosaurs are just as common. Visitors to museums often think that the dinosaurs walked around looking like living skeletons! Politicians and writers sometimes unfairly use dinosaurs to describe something that is old-fashioned, out of date, useless, or inefficient. It is common to think that dinosaurs were big, dull, stupid, and headed for extinction because they were poorly designed to cope with the world in which they lived. In fact, nothing could be further from the truth. Dinosaurs were among the most elegant and sophisticated animals that the Earth has ever seen. They survived for nearly 150 million years - 75 times longer than humans have lived on Earth.

DINOSAUR DRAGON
The winged dragon of mythology looks a lot like some dinosaurs, except for the wings. Some people see dragons and dinosaurs as being one and the same. But the big difference is that dragons never existed!

A WATERY END
A common misbelief is that dinosaurs were sea monsters, possibly still lurking in the ocean depths. In fact, no dinosaur was purely sea living. The sea reptiles that shared the dinosaur world were mostly plesiosaurs and ichthyosaurs.

DINOSAURS IN THE TREES
When *Hypsilophodon*, a small, agile, plant-eating dinosaur, was first discovered, it was thought to live in trees. In fact, it was believed to be the dinosaur equivalent of a tree kangaroo that lives in Papua New Guinea. Scientists thought its long tail helped it to balance in the trees, and special sharp toes on its feet helped it to cling to branches. Now this theory has been proved wrong. In fact, *Hypsilophodon* was a ground-dwelling dinosaur that used its stiff tail as a stabilizer while running.

THE GREAT BRONTOSAURUS HOAX
The sauropod dinosaur *Apatosaurus* used to be called *Brontosaurus*. Its almost complete skeleton was dug up, lacking only a skull. When it came to reconstructing the animal, its fossil bones got mixed up with another sauropod, *Camarasaurus*, and it appeared in museums with a short and round skull. It was not until recently that the original skull was found, proving to be a lot like the skull of *Diplodocus* (p. 22).

wo *Hypsilophodon* dinosaurs perched in a tree

Special grasping toes

Balancing tail

Grasping hand to hold branch

DINOSAURS AND CAVE DWELLERS
Some films and cartoons have given the impression that dinosaurs shared the Earth with early people. In fact, dinosaurs became extinct 64 million years before the first people ever appeared on the Earth!

Index

A

Albertosaurus, 60
Allosaurus, 23
ammonites, 48, 60
amphibians, 56
Anatosaurus, 28
ankylosaurs (armored dinosaurs), 20, 21, 22, 27, 32, 33
Apatosaurus, 12, 43, 62
Archaeopteryx, 50, 51
armadillo, 32, 33
armor, 22, 32, 33, 59
armored dinosaurs (ankylosaurs), 20, 21

B

Baryonyx, 43, 53, 55
beetles, 56
birds, 22, 29, 44, 48, 50, 51, 58, 59
birth of dinosaurs, 46
bones, 6, 8, 9, 12, 16, 17, 29, 33, 34, 37, 40, 42, 54,
brachiopods, 61
Brachiosaurus, 12
brain, 35
Brontosaurus, 62

C

Camarasaurus, 19, 62
camouflage, 21, 32
Captorhinus, 56
carnivores (meat eaters), 23, 33, 36, 38
carnosaurs, 24-25, 34
ceratopsians (horned dinosaurs), 19, 26, 30-31, 44, 46
Ceratosaurus, 25
chevron bones, 18, 19, 34, 35
claws, 42-43
cockroach, 59
coelacanth, 56

Coelophysis, 50, 51
coelurosaurs, 24
Compsognathus, 12, 13, 37, 50, 51
conifers, 10, 11, 14, 23, 26
Corythosaurus, 28, 38
crab, 60
Cretaceous Period, 56, 59, 60, 61
crocodiles, 7, 20, 32, 48, 57, 58, 59
cycads, 10, 11, 14, 26, 27, 57

D

deadly nightshade, 48
defense, 14, 20, 21, 25, 28, 30, 33, 35, 42
Deinonychus, 19, 42, 43
digestion, 26
Diictodon, 56
Dimetrodon, 35
Diplodocus, 14-21, 23, 33, 38, 43, 46, 62
discovery of dinosaurs, 8
dogwood, 11
dragonfly, 58
Dryosaurus, 59
duckbilled dinosaurs (hadrosaurs) 10, 21, 26, 27, 28, 45, 46

E

Echinodon, 26
Edmontosaurus, 27
eggs, 44-45, 46, 48
Euoplocephalus, 20, 21,
Euparkeria, 7
extinction, 6, 48-49, 60

F

feeding, 14, 22
ferns, 10, 11, 27
fish, 58, 60
flowering plants, 10, 11
footprints, 40
forests, 10, 11, 14

fossils, 6, 8, 9, 13, 22, 30, 32, 40, 44, 48, 50, 51, 52-53, 54, 55, 56, 57, 58, 63

G

Gallimimus, 36
gastroliths, 26
gastropod, 59
ginkgo, 11, 50,
giraffes, 14
Gorgosaurus, 25
grey plover, 58
growth of dinosaurs, 46, 47
Gryodus, 58

H

hadrosaurs (duckbilled dinosaurs), 26, 28, 38, 49
hands, 38-39
Hawkins, Benjamin Waterhouse, 9, 55
heads, 28-29
herbivores (plant eaters), 10, 21, 23, 36, 38
Heterodontosaurus, 36
hip bones, 6, 18, 49, 51
hoatzin, 51
holly, 11
horned dinosaurs (ceratopsians), 14, 19, 30-31
horses, 61
horsetail, 10, 11, 27,
humans, 22, 27, 61
Hylaeosaurus, 8
Hypsilophodon, 36, 37, 62, 63
Hyracotherium, 61

IJK

ichthyosaurs, 48, 57, 60, 62
Iguanodon, 6, 8, 9, 25, 27, 39, 40, 49, 54, 59

iguana, 6, 7, 8, 26
insects, 13, 24, 51, 61
Jurassic Period, 56, 58, 59
kangaroo, 18
king crab, 58

L

laurel, 11
legs, 6, 16, 36-39
lions, 25
lizards, 6, 13, 20, 31, 32, 58, 59, 60, 61
see also iguana
lobster, 60
lungfish, 56

M

magnolias, 11
Maiasaura, 44, 46
Mamenchiasaurus, 14, 15
mammals, 24, 60
Mantell, Dr Gideon, 8, 9
Mantell, Mary Ann, 8
marsupials, 60
Massetognathus, 57
Massospondylus, 23, 42
meat eaters (carnivores), 14, 19, 20, 22, 23, 24-25, 30, 32, 42, 43, 50
Megalosaurus, 8, 25
Megazostrodon, 57
monkey puzzle trees, 11
Morosaurus, 19
Mosasaurus, 52
mosasaurs, 48, 60
muscles, 15, 18, 19, 54

NO

neck, 14, 15
nests, 44-45, 46
Nuthetes, 25
omnivores, 23, 42, 57
ornithischian dinosaurs, 6
Ornithomimus, 42
Ornithosuchus, 7
ostrich, 36, 37

Owen, Sir Richard, 8

P

Pachycephalosaurus, 28, 29
paleontologist, 52, 53
Parasaurolophus, 10, 28, 29
passionflower, 11
pine trees, 26, 27
plant eaters (herbivores), 12, 20, 22, 23, 26, 30, 34, 39, 42,
plants, 10, 11, 23, 26, 29, 60, 61
Plateosaurus, 39
plesiosaurs, 48, 58, 62
Polacanthus, 32
Procolophon, 56
Proterosuchus, 7
Protoceratops, 31, 44, 45, 46, 47
Psittacosaurus, 29
Pterodactylus, 58
pterosaurs, 6, 22, 48, 58, 59

QR

quail, 44
rhinoceroses, 30
Riojasuchus, 57
rodents, 61

S

saurischian dinosaurs, 6
sauropods, 11, 12, 13, 18, 19, 20, 21, 26, 27, 33, 46
Scelidosaurus, 20, 38,
scorpions, 56
sedimentary rock, 52
sharks, 61
skin, 32, 54
sloth, 8
Smith, William, 9
snakes, 59
Staurikosaurus, 7
stegosaurs (plated dinosaurs), 20, 21, 34-35
Stegosaurus, 11, 21, 34, 35

Struthiomimus, 36
Styracosaurus, 44
Supersaurus, 12

T

tails: uses, 18-21
teeth, 6, 8, 10, 22, 23, 24-25, 26, 27, 29, 36, 59
thecodonts, 7, 57
Thecodontosaurus, 57
theropoda, 24
toe bones, 38, 40
trace fossils, 40
Triassic Period, 56
Triceratops, 6, 14, 26, 30-31, 38
trilobite, 56
Troodon, 24
tuatara, 7
Tuojiangosaurus, 34-35
turtles, 60, 61
tyrannosaurus rex, 6, 14, 24, 30, 38, 39, 49,

UWY

Ultrasaurus, 12
wishbone, 50
yew, 26

Acknowledgments

Dorling Kindersley would like to thank:
Angela Milner and the staff of the British Museum (Natural History); Kew Gardens and Clifton Nurseries for advice and plant specimens for photography; Trevor Smith's Animal World; The Institute of Vertebrate Palaeoanthropology, Beijing, for permission to photograph Chinese dinosaurs; Brian Carter for obtaining plant specimens; Victoria Sorzano for typing; William Lindsay for advice on pages 52-53 and pages 54-55; Fred Ford and Mike Pilley of Radius Graphics; Jane Parker for the index; Richard Czapnik for design assistance; and Dave King for special photography on pages 6-7 and pages 10-11.

Picture credits
t=top, b=bottom, m=middle, l=left, r=right
ANT/ NHPA: 7tr
BBC Hulton Picture Library: 8tl, 9tm, 31t, 54tl, 54b
Richard Beales/Planet Earth Pictures: 32tl
The Bridgeman Art Library: 17bl
The British Museum (Natural History): 52tl, 52ml, 55tl
Zdenek Burian/Artia Foreign Trade Corporation: 10m, 22m, 38tl
Jane Burton/Bruce Coleman Limited: 6ml, 13br, 29ml, 34tl, 35tl, 36tl, 39tr, 43bl, 50tl, 57bl, 59tl
L. Castaneda/ The Image Bank: 15mr
Albert Dickson: 46bl
Robert Harding: 63tr
David A. Hardy/ Science Photo Library: 49tl
Arthur Hayward/Natural Science Photos: 11ml, 24tr, 29bl, 33tr, 37tr, 42bl
The Illustrated London News: 38ml, 46tl,

G. Kinns/Natural Science Photos: 30tl
Kobal Collection: 63m
Ken Lucas/ Planet Earth Pictures: 31mr
The Mansell Collection: 28tl, 42mr, 56tr,
Mary Evans Picture Library: 9bl, 9m, 12tl, 14tl, 16bl, 25ml, 34ml, 35bm, 62tl, 62bl, 62mr
David Norman: 53mr
Alan Root/ Survival Anglia Ltd: 51tr
C. A. Walker/ Natural Science Photos: 40tl

Illustrations by: Angelika Elsebach for pp. 21tr, 21mr, 21br, 36b; Sandie Hill for pp. 15ml, 20ml, 28tr, 44tr, 44bl; Mark Iley for p. 18bl; Richard Ward for pp. 23bl, 26bm, 47b; Ann Winterbotham for pp. 10tl, 15bl; John Woodcock for pp. 6tr, 7mr, 12m, 14b, 14ml 51b, 54br

Picture research by: Angela Murphy